SONG OF BE

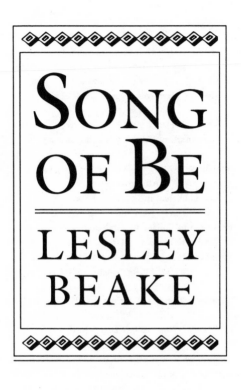

SONG OF BE

LESLEY BEAKE

HENRY HOLT AND COMPANY · NEW YORK

Henry Holt and Company, Inc.
Publishers since 1866
115 West 18th Street
New York, New York 10011

Henry Holt is a registered
trademark of Henry Holt and Company, Inc.

First published in the United States in 1993 by
Henry Holt and Company, Inc.
Published in Canada by Fitzhenry & Whiteside Ltd.,
195 Allstate Parkway, Markham, Ontario L3R 4T8.
Originally published in South Africa in 1991 by
Maskew Miller Longman (Pty) Ltd.

Library of Congress Cataloging-in-Publication Data
Beake Lesley.
Song of Be / Lesley Beake.
p.   cm.—(Edge books)
Summary: Be, a young Bushman woman searching in the
desert for the peace she remembers from her childhood,
realizes that she and her people must reconcile new personal
and political realities with ancient traditions.
[1. San (African people)—Fiction. 2. Africa—Fiction.]
I. Title. II. Series.
PZ7.B3568So 1993 [Fic]—dc20 93-11440

ISBN 0-8050-2905-2

First American Edition—1993

Designed by Victoria Hartman

Printed in the United States of America
on acid-free paper. ∞
3 5 7 9 10 8 6 4 2

In memory of my grandmothers,
Millie Condon
and Isabella Dewar

ACKNOWLEDGMENTS

My special thanks go to Megan Biesele and Claire Ritchie of the Ju/'hoan Bushman Development Foundation for their help and encouragement and, most of all, for their friendship.

The members of the Nyae Nyae Farmers' Cooperative generously allowed me to sit in on their meetings and discussions, from which I learned a great deal.

I am grateful also to the many Ju/'hoan people who permitted me to watch them going about their daily business, and cheerfully submitted to photographs by yet another outsider.

The staff of the Windhoek Reference Library patiently sifted through piles of books until I found the information I needed.

Thank you all.

AUTHOR'S NOTE
About the Time and Place of This Book

There is a part of Africa called Namibia. It lies between the cold Atlantic Ocean and the dry deserts of the Namib and the Kalahari, a huge stretch of land where fewer than two million people live, fishermen and farmers, and miners who fight with the sea for the diamonds found along the empty beaches of the west coast.

This new nation only recently became independent and the people there are fiercely proud of their country. The last few years have been a time of change in many ways as the many different groups learn to speak with new voices and make their feelings heard.

Men and women who had never before been consulted about the way their country should be governed were suddenly included. They were asked to vote in the first democratic election that Namibia had ever had, and the United Nations came to watch, and monitor, and make sure that those elections were indeed free and fair.

It was an exciting time to be in Namibia.

In the north of Namibia, and far to the east, is an area known as Nyae Nyae, which is part of the great

Kalahari Desert. This is not desert as we often imagine it. There are no great sweeping sand dunes, and there is sometimes water to be found if you have the skill to look for it. Many types of thorn trees grow here, as well as the tall, strange baobab trees, which look as if they have been planted upside down, with their roots in the air. White-gold grass bends in the hot wind, and there are fruits and berries, roots and tubers, which provide food—and liquid too—for those who are hungry and thirsty.

Tracks crisscross the Kalahari Desert where men and animals walk and where four-wheel-drive vehicles churn through the dust in summer and the mud in winter. Often, if you travel when the summer rains have fallen heavy on the land, you must drive off the place where the track used to be, because an elephant has wallowed in the mud and churned up what used to be the road.

As you pass, sable antelope and springbok stop to watch you or scamper away with a flick of their tails. Giraffe lurch across the landscape, browsing on the taller thorn trees, and in the grass a million tiny creatures forage and feed. Lions prowl at night, taking the people's cattle and donkeys if they are not shut up in a walled enclosure. This is Nyae Nyae.

There are people here, too. The Ju/'hoan people. They have been here for a very long time, driven away from the other parts of Africa where they once lived, to this place, where they have learned the skills that make survival possible.

Much has been written about these people, who are sometimes called the San, but who prefer to be known as the Bushmen. They are hunter-gatherers who understand the balance of the land and the plants and animals they find on it. For many years they have crossed the Kalahari in family groups, collecting and hunting, and living their lives.

But no place is isolated from the twentieth century, and nothing stands still forever. Other people came to the Kalahari, and they brought change—not always good change.

Farmers came, wishing to find cheap labor. War came, and the Ju/'hoan were taken away from their own place, their n!ores, and employed as trackers in the armed forces. Transistor radios came, bringing news. Traders came, bringing sugar and washing powder and bottles of brandy. Other wandering peoples came, wanting to graze their cattle on Ju/'hoan land, and government officials came, bringing rules and regulations. Change came.

If you go to Nyae Nyae today, you will find the Ju/'hoan in a challenging stage of their history. The way of life that is shown in the glossy picture books is gone forever, and the people of Nyae Nyae have paid a heavy price with its passing. But there is a future for the Ju/'hoan—something that the old people began to doubt. The Bushmen are going back to their traditional lands and they are learning the new skills that they need.

They still hunt when they have the chance, but they also buy meat when they travel to town in four-wheel-drive vehicles. They still collect and eat the Kalahari food, but they grow vegetables too in the village gardens, and keep cattle for milk. They still know where to find water in the desert, but they have wind pumps that bring sweet water to the surface from deep underground.

The Bushmen have never thought of themselves as a people or tribe, and have always functioned as loose family groups who regarded a certain area of land, or n!ore, as their own. But now, recognizing the need to be heard, they have organized a group to speak for them. The Nyae Nyae Farmers' Cooperative makes their voices heard at national government level and even abroad. The Ju/'hoan are going to survive, as a group, as a people with their own identity, as contributors to the twenty-first century.

SONG OF BE

The smoke in the flames
of the fires of Bushmanland.
The honey-gold of the grass
and the wind singing through.
The scent of sweetness on the air
and the soft, gray dust
—before our footsteps
were blown out.

SONG
OF BE

1

I have just killed myself.

I meant it to be quick, but when I came to stick the poison arrow into the vein in my arm, I couldn't, and the arrow tip went into the thickest part of my leg instead. Maybe, inside my head, I wanted a little more time. To think.

So I am sitting here under the thin shade of a thorn tree and thinking about my life and the things that were me—Be, of the Ju/'hoan people.

◆ The first thing I remember . . . is smoke. That was the first thing. Warm, gray smoke rising from a small fire with an orange flame. The warmth was not just from the fire—hot on my feet and warm on my legs— but from behind me as well, the warmth of the people and smoky blankets. The warmth of love.

It surrounded me so that I was full and complete, with the happiness of belonging deep inside me. Aia was there. I remember feeling her presence, somewhere on the other side of the circle, but I didn't need my own mother close to me to have happiness. If Aia was busy, or out gathering food in the veld, or away somewhere else, there were other people to love me almost as much.

3

Their voices enclosed me. Deep voices of the old people and small voices of the young ones playing behind the fire-circle. Somebody was singing softly a little way off. The dogs and puppies and chickens kept getting in the way and once the old rooster ran right over old Kamha and everyone laughed—old Kamha most of all.

I remember times when we went to the veld to find food; the sound of the women calling to one another and their laughter. I remember Aia walking ahead of me and my looking up to her, walking with a straight back.

I remember coming home late, over the veld, with the warm dusty sunshine in our eyes and tsama melons in our arms and in the women's carrying bags. We could see the small smoke from the cooking fires where the old ones waited, and hear the barking of the dogs who had recognized us while we were still far away. Then the sun would be red in the low sky and the people would come from where they had been— from hunting, or from the vegetable gardens—and they would sit together and smoke and talk.

A time comes to my mind that I thought I had forgotten. Xama went to get water at the wind pump. The sky was bright, bright blue, and the grass and the thorn trees were green with summer and the air warm with it.

My friend Nisa came with us and she and I also had small buckets to bring back water. Our feet danced and danced in the dust and the honey scent of the bush was around us. We passed the place where the old baobab tree is, and the birds whirled and whirred around our heads when they heard us laughing.

"Wash!" old Xama said when we got to the water

4

hole where the cattle drink. She took Nisa's green dress and my red dress and tramped them in the tub she had brought with the other washing. Nisa and I played in the water and the cool drops flew through the air like bright beads, cold on our skin.

On that night—or another night, I don't know now—I remember the smell of the new grass that Aia and her friends had used to thatch our small hut, and the feel of the smooth, gray dust between my toes. I remember the kudu skin that Aia used to cover me with when I went to sleep, soft and supple from being worked and worked between her fingers.

"Good night, child," she said, and her voice was love. "Good night, my child. Sleep now, under the stars."

Through the opening of the hut I could see them—many, many bright and shining lights, scattered over the dark sky of Bushmanland.

I drifted into sleep, and our people were around me like a hum, like bees, soft and warm, and honey scented.

I know now why we had to go to my grandfather in the Gobabis District. Then I didn't.

We went on foot at first and my feet dragged in the dust behind Aia's footprints and I was hot and tired and wanted to go home.

"I want to go home!" I can still hear the words in my young voice as well as the silence before Aia spoke.

"There is no home now, Be. Now we must go on, to another place. We must do this for my father, who needs us."

I didn't understand. How could I?

We walked and walked, a long, long time. The bush

5

through which our feet led us was thick. Thorns pulled at my skirt and worried their way into my skin so that Aia had to stop and help me before we went on.

"When will we get there?"

But Aia had no answer, just a sigh that might have been the wind.

I was afraid of the lions. Always we had been told, Nisa and I, to be careful of the lions.

"Don't go out of the village on your own!"

"Don't wander off into the veld!"

"Stay with the older children, they will watch over you."

The big people didn't always say the word, but we children knew what they were thinking of: lions.

"What about the lions, Aia?"

Aia sighed again, saying: "They will come if they come. I will make a fire at night."

Somehow that didn't seem like enough protection to me, but no lions came and we didn't even hear their voices, shouting to one another in the darkness. I know that because I listened.

We came to a place with buildings that were made out of bricks and had roofs of tin. There was a shop where people were buying flour and mealie meal and tobacco, but Aia didn't go in.

"We have our food," she said, patting her carrying bag, which hung over her shoulder, "and we have no money for such things."

I remember turning back to look, after we had passed that place, and there was a small girl, like me, looking as well. She had on a blue dress that was so dirty it was almost gray, and a red tin in her hand from which she was drinking. She didn't speak, but her eyes made her

6

my friend. I would have liked to stay with her and maybe go to her hut and speak of things that we might know.

I was so tired. Aia carried me for a time when my feet couldn't carry me anymore. She tied me on her back with her kudu blanket as she had done when I was a small child, and balanced her bundle on her head. Aia was used to carrying heavy loads—she did that every day when she went gathering in the veld—but I could feel through her skin how tired she was and soon I asked to be put down so that I could walk and maybe help her a little.

"Can I sing to you, Aia?"

Aia smiled her special smile that I loved. "Yes, Be, child of my heart, sing for me."

For a time I sang the songs that I knew from our fireside and our people, but I began to feel the sadness choking my words, and Aia too was quiet and still as she walked. I stopped singing then.

"Why do we have to go?"

Aia thought for a moment, as if she wasn't sure what to say. "My father—who is your grandfather—works for a white farmer in the south. He has worked there for most of the years of his life."

I waited while she thought again.

"Last week Gumtsa brought me a message. It said . . ."

Aia's voice trailed away as if she didn't want to hear the words she was about to say. ". . . it said that we must come. My father is old and sick, and he needs me to help him with his work."

Then Aia pressed her lips together in a way that told me she wasn't going to say any more right then.

* * *

It was the dry time, but Aia knew where to look for the food that would give us water and fill our stomachs. She examined the ground carefully while we walked, for this was not a familiar place where she knew every bush and the cycle of every plant. When she found tsama melons or tsi beans or sweet nin berries, she would put them carefully inside her carrying bag for later. We had four ostrich shells filled with water and plugged with grass, and we had some sticks of dried meat which Tushay had given us before we started our journey.

"I do not like this," Tushay said. "But maybe you must go." And he looked at Aia a long time as if there were other things that he might have said. Then we left.

Aia would watch the sun as it moved over our heads and feel the breeze that came from the west, and her footsteps were sure in the dust as we made our way south.

The walk lasted many days. At night Aia made a big fire, in case of the lions. I had a little shelter to sleep in, built with branches and Aia's carrying skin, but through it I could still see the stars, which were the same as they had been in our own place, scattered like dust across the black.

Aia sat at her fire and I could feel that her thoughts were lonely ones. I remember looking, one night, for the last time before my eyes fell closed, seeing her shape, dark against the yellow of the flames, bent forward as if she was listening to something that only she could hear.

In the morning Aia woke me and her smile was back.

"Come, Be. It is time to walk again. Soon we will be with your grandfather."

I had never met Grandfather. While I walked, I thought about what he would be like. What would the place be like? What would our lives be like when we got there?

It was hard for me to think those things, because I had never been anywhere except our home. Maybe he would live in a house like we had seen in that village, with a tin roof and brick walls. Maybe he would have a lot of money so that we could buy things in a shop and Aia wouldn't have to work so hard to find food.

After a long time we saw a donkey cart. Aia and I rode in the back, and the dirt under the wheels shook and shook and shook us, until our teeth rattled in our heads, and we were glad to get back down again, even though our feet were still tired.

Once a blue truck stopped. The driver was a black man who smiled, showing his white teeth, and spoke to Aia in words I didn't understand, but he was kind. The other people sitting with him in the front waved at us with their arms, indicating that we must get on, so we climbed into the back, where there were cans of petrol and diesel. The truck flew over the bumpy road and the cold wind bit our ears until it was time for us to climb down and start to walk again.

And then we came to Ontevrede.

"Now," Aia said, "is the time to stop being a child and to learn new things."

I wondered what the new things would be.

There was a green board at the gate, with the name of the farm. Aia stood for a long moment, just looking at it. "What does it say?" she asked me.

"Ontevrede," I told her.

Aia nodded her head. "Yes, Ontevrede," and that was all she said until we had walked up the long, dusty road that led to a white house with four tall, dark trees around it.

Some Herero people were standing waiting for pay when we arrived, so it must have been a Friday evening. Their eyes measured us as we walked across the yard.

"Good day," Aia said quietly.

They looked at us without smiling, but their faces were not unfriendly. "Good day," said one. "Why have you come with this child?"

"I am looking for my father, who is called Dam."

All the Herero people smiled then, or laughed. "Ah. The Bushman." I didn't like the way they said that, as if our people were not good enough for them.

"Yes. My father is a Bushman, and so are we." Aia's head went up when she said that and she was proud.

One of the Herero men, who I know now was called Moses, answered quite kindly then. "Dam will be at the back. He hasn't finished with the feed yet." Moses jerked his head in the way that we should go and Aia thanked him. I could feel their eyes on us when we went.

The shed was full of cows, brown and black, and one with a gray hide and white spots who looked at me with her yellow eyes when I passed. The smell was of cattle dung and straw and warmth, and I thought I would like to lie down quietly beside that gray cow and sleep and sleep in her straw. At the end of the shed was Grandfather, shoveling hay into the feed troughs.

"Father?" There was a question in Aia's voice. "Father? We have come, as your message, which Gumtsa brought, asked us to."

I was surprised. Grandfather was old, much older than I had imagined. His face was very wrinkled and lined. The skin on his arms hung in folds as if it had become too large for him. He was so thin. . . .

And then Grandfather smiled. I think it was worth all the hard walking and riding in donkey carts and trucks when we saw the happiness in Grandfather's face. He dropped the fork he was using and just stood and looked and looked at us as if he would never have enough of looking.

"Thank you," he said and he took my hand and that of Aia in his and we were together.

Sitting here, under my thorn tree, I am watching the sun move slowly across the afternoon sky. I am not sorry that it is finished, that it is over. There were too many hard things.

After we had seen Grandfather, we saw Kleinbaas. I didn't know why he was called by a name that means "small boss" because he is very big. His shadow stretched right across the cow shed when he came in at the door behind Grandfather.

"Dam? Haven't you finished yet?" His voice, which now I know well, was not angry, but like it almost always is, tired and irritated with everyone and everything. His voice wasn't a big voice, but one that belonged to a small person with a small mind.

Grandfather made himself taller. His shoulders went back and he put down the hayfork he was holding.

"I have nearly finished," Grandfather said. "I have

11

just stopped to welcome my daughter and my granddaughter, who have come, as I said to you they would."

Kleinbaas peered at us in the gloom of the cow shed. I could hear the cows behind me, chewing softly, their hooves moving on the concrete floor.

"Hmm," Kleinbaas said. He was thick and pink and solid, and his legs stood steady in their long blue socks and brown leather shoes, as if they were planted there and could not be moved.

He looked mostly at Aia. His eyes slid very quickly over me, as if I wasn't important. "You worked in a kitchen before?" he said to Aia. He spoke quickly with short, sharp words.

"No, sir, I have not," Aia said, "but I can learn."

"And milking? Do you know about milking? I'll expect you to help out after the housework's done. It shouldn't take you all day. There's only the two of us."

"Yes, sir, I know about milking."

Again there was that quiet, and again I heard the sounds of the cows.

"And mending? There's always stuff to be mended at Ontevrede." Kleinbaas laughed shortly.

"Yes."

"Hmm. We'll see. There's no place for loafers at Ontevrede. No place for loafers at all. We work hard here."

Aia did not answer this time, and Grandfather too was silent.

"I only agreed to keep this tired old man on because he promised me he would get someone *reliable* to help in the house and with . . . with . . . other things that need to be done."

Nobody said anything back to Kleinbaas, so he went on by himself.

"I run a tight operation here. Ontevrede isn't one of those fancy farms like you get down south. Not like in the Cape, where my brother . . ."

Kleinbaas stopped there and his look was bitter. "Not like that lot down there. This is hard country and a man has to be hard to make a living. You understand me?"

Aia nodded.

"My wife is . . . not always well." Kleinbaas stopped again and for the first time I felt that there was something gentle about this man, after all his hard, sharp words.

"She needs help. In the house, you understand."

But that was not really what Kleinbaas meant when he said that.

"I'll give you a week to learn—no pay, but food and a room. Then we'll see."

Aia nodded again and he turned to go. But then he came back and when he spoke his voice was slow, like jam sticking to a spoon. "I'm not a bad man," he said, and then he was gone. I wondered who he was really trying to say those words to.

Kleinbaas had another name, which was Mr. Coetzee, but none of us on the farm called him that. Mrs. Coetzee was small and pretty, and very thin, and her eyes didn't always look at you when she was speaking. Her hair was beautiful, long and yellow and shiny. She was wearing a soft blue dress that first day, with a small white collar. Her hands kept going to the collar and touching it, as if she wasn't certain whether it was

13

still there or not, and her hands were long and thin with short-cut nails and the ring of Kleinbaas shining on one of her fingers.

Her own name, which I always called her in my mind, was Min. It was a good name for her, light and soft and . . . I don't know what I mean to say, but Min's name was almost said before the word was made and Min was like that, too.

"What are your names?" she said to Aia when we went to the back door of the farmhouse. "What would you like me to call you?"

Aia told Min our names. She nodded. "Good." Her eyes looked past our faces to where the sky was gold and red with the last of the sun. "There is a room. . . ." She took some keys from a hook behind the door. She didn't tell us to follow her, but we went anyway, across the farmyard, where the Herero men were collecting their pay from Kleinbaas in small brown envelopes. Grandfather was there too, so he must have finished with the feed. He smiled at me when I passed.

"It's not much. . . ." Min waved her hands in a helpless way. "I keep meaning to do something about the rooms, but there never seems to be . . ."

The room was in a row of other rooms, damp and dark and narrow, with a dirty window, too high from which to see. The floor was cold concrete and there was a single bed in one corner and a cardboard box in another.

"Maybe tomorrow . . . I could take out some old curtains perhaps and find a few bits and pieces . . ."

Min smiled at Aia, but I thought suddenly that she wasn't happy, not in her mind nor in her voice. That didn't seem right when she had Kleinbaas, who was a powerful man, and the big house with all the things in it that I had seen when we were standing at the door.

Hundreds of things, there were, all shining bright and clean. There were also pots on the windowsill with plants growing in them and there was the smell of food and coffee. There was a radio, like the one Hau brought back with him after he worked for the government that time, and there was warmth and safety. How could she be unhappy?

When I was still very young, I thought like that. It was then that I thought what you *had* was important. Now I know that it is what you *are*.

If only . . . but those are words that I should take from my head and throw away. I have said them too often, and thought them in my mind, and whispered them in the dark, dark nights. Now it is too late for "if only."

Shall I light a fire? How long will the poison take to work? Once I ate from a giraffe that had been shot with a poison arrow. Four days, they said, it took to die, and all the time the men from our village followed it, waiting for it to fall. Then they cut out the soft parts that would go bad quickly and ate them, cooked over a fire.

We all feasted that night when the meat was brought home, carried on the backs of the hunters. It was divided up, as it always is, in the correct way. Tushay, as the maker of the arrow, had the best meat. The man who fired the arrow had the next choice, and then the rest was divided up among the other hunters, who gave it to their families and parents-in-law and friends. Aia had part of a leg and we scraped the slivers of meat clean from the bone, and then boiled the bone, to make a soup. Tushay, who lived in the hut next door, had the head, which he baked in a deep pit of ash. I can still smell it.

16

How long will a small person take to die? Four days is a long time. Maybe I should gather some berries or bulbs from the veld. Maybe I should cook some tsama melon soup over the fire and eat it and pretend that I don't have the poison from the arrow inside my blood. Yes, maybe I should do that.

Will my death hurt a lot, I wonder?

◈ That night, the first night on Ontevrede, I slept beside Aia in the narrow bed. There were two new blankets, red and blue, and red and green, which Min had given us, and Aia folded them neatly over us. Their smell was very strong and new and I missed Aia's soft leather in which she used to wrap me. The smell of those blankets seemed to smother out the feeling of the place and there were no stars in the small, high window. Aia didn't move when she cried, but I felt her, through her skin.

Ontevrede, I know now, is a cattle farm deep in the Gobabis District, about three hours by truck from the nearest village. Thorn bushes are everywhere around it, and the grass is white in the winter when all the water has dried out of it, and pale green in the summer months when the thunder comes with the rains. There are a lot of cattle—five thousand of them. I know that because Kleinbaas often said it.

"Five thousand head of cattle," he would say, "and every one a winner!"

That was when he was in a good mood. Other times he was angry.

"Five thousand head of cattle," he would say then, "and every one a bloody nuisance!"

Kleinbaas talked a lot, just to himself as if we weren't there, so we always knew what he was thinking.

"Bushmen," he would say when he was pleased, "best workers I've ever had on Ontevrede!"

Other times, when he was not pleased, he said different things.

Grandfather worked with the tractors, and the welding machine that spat blue fire, and a portable generator that went "Tereketere-wah-wah" all the time it was on. Grandfather was very lined and wrinkled but he smiled a lot. He also coughed a lot.

"He's *been* to the TB clinic," Kleinbaas said defensively. "And he's *had* the pills. I made sure he took them, too."

I had the feeling that Kleinbaas would miss Grandfather if he ever went away.

"Been here for . . . oh, must be more than forty years," Kleinbaas said. "Since long before I used to come here as a kid. Never missed a day—even when he was sick."

Kleinbaas was proud of Grandfather and the way he had learned to work the welding machine, which was something Kleinbaas said the Hereros never managed to do. "Always breaking the bloody thing," he said, and he and Grandfather exchanged a kind of grin that made me think they were friends in a way.

"Good learners," Kleinbaas said about Bushmen. That was after Aia had been in the kitchen for a week and Min was pleased with her. "Always said so. Pick anything up if you just take the trouble to teach them." And then he said again the bit about how Bushmen were the best workers he'd ever had on Ontevrede. "Dirty, of course," he added. "Can't expect miracles, though."

Kleinbaas was always pink and clean, with blue

shorts and a white shirt and long pale blue socks that came up to his knees. Aia washed all these things for him in the tub outside the kitchen door and then hung them up on the old wire that stretched between two poles. Sometimes, when she had a few minutes' rest, she would wash our things as well and then they smelled of sun and of the blue powder Min measured out, using the old tin mug every morning.

We lived and we lived. I am trying to think how long it was, this time, in the beginning at Ontevrede. It was winter when we came there. I remember that because of the food in the veld being hard to find when we left our village. Then I remember it being very hot, in the time before the rains, but I don't know if that was the same year or another year. And then there were maybe two more rains, maybe three. Aia never knew the numbers of years. She remembered important things that had happened, not numbers.

"That was the year when the trophy hunters brought the elephant meat," she would say.

"That was the year when old Hau broke his leg and had to go to the hospital in Grootfontein on the back of the magistrate's truck.

"That was the year when the small rain didn't come and we were hungry."

Sometimes, when she was remembering, she would smile. "That was the year you were born, Be."

And this was the year that I became a woman.

Aia was pleased. But she was also sad. "There should be other women," she said. "There should be special dancing, and a hut where you stay, and the people

19

should be happy because there is another woman among them."

Then Aia was quiet for a little while.

She told Kleinbaas I was sick and she made me stay in our room. I lay and I thought about many things. Then, on the fourth day, when I had finished becoming a woman, for that time, Aia brought oil and made my skin gleam with it, and beads which she said she had kept for me and special food which we ate together so that my stomach was full and I was happy that at last I was grown.

For a time we were silent.

"What was it like?" I said at last. "When I was born?"

"Pain," Aia said. "I had not known there would be so much pain."

"I'm sorry," I told her. My voice was very quiet.

Aia smiled. "Oh, no," she said, "*you* don't have to be sorry, my Be. When you were born . . ." Aia folded her arms over her stomach as if she was remembering.

"When you were about to be born, I woke in the night. 'Eh!' I thought. 'But I am sick!' And then I thought, 'No. This is my child. This is my baby.' "

Aia looked at me. "Do you know what I did?"

"No, Aia."

"Do you know what I thought?"

I shook my head.

"I thought that you were so . . . special, that I would not call for the old women to come. I would go *myself* and I would have *my* child on *my* own. That's what I thought."

Between Aia and me, at that moment, was a cord that was stronger than the birth cord. I felt it.

"I covered your father—he was still sleeping—with my kaross and I went out into the night.

"Oh, Be. The stars, the night you were born, the stars!"

For a moment Aia and I were both quiet, then she went on.

"There were more stars than grains of sand which I could hold in my two hands. I watched them, when the pain came, and they sang to me—such music!

"The pain pulled and pulled me from deep in the earth, but every time I looked up, the music took my heart away. Took my heart away. Until you were born, my Be.

"I lay there for a long time, listening to the stars, and you lay with me, until they came to find me and I heard their voices calling and calling. I didn't shout back. I just lay there and *we* were together.

"They came then, and greeted you with lovely names, and cut the cord and buried the afterbirth, and carried us home to where it was warm and safe.

"I lay in our hut—and the stars still sang."

That was a year I remember, but the other years of Ontevrede were all one, until the end.

I think I must be fourteen or fifteen now, by the years Min taught me, but I'm not really sure.

Min was my friend from the beginning. On that first morning Aia was very busy in the kitchen. It looked different from when we had arrived. There were pots and dishes and plates and cups everywhere.

"This is the washing-up liquid," Min said. Aia looked . . . well, helpless. She looked smaller and thinner than she had been, as if all the bright, shining things in the kitchen had drained away some of herself.

"Do you understand?" Min asked.

Aia looked afraid.

Min took the plastic bottle then and turned on the tap so that the hot water ran and the steam misted up the glass on the window.

"Look, you put in a squeeze of this soap." Min did that, and there were bubbles everywhere in the water. "And then you start with the glasses." Min put some of the glasses in the water. "And then the plates . . . and then the pots." Min touched all these things lightly as she spoke. "Until they are all done."

Aia started to wash the glasses and Min looked pleased. "Be will come and brush my hair."

That was one of Min's good days, when her eyes were looking at things and her voice was strong. She took me to a room with sunshine-yellow curtains that blew gently in the open window, and a neat bed with a white cover and two dolls sitting on it. Min saw me looking at the dolls and she held one out for me to see, but not close enough for me to touch.

"My children," she said, and her eyes were sad. "Now . . . brush!"

I brushed and brushed her long golden hair with a silver brush and all the while Min talked, although I didn't understand everything she said.

Before we went to Ontevrede there was a class at the camp, where the foreign people were, and they taught the children from our village, but I only got to Book Two before I met Min, so I couldn't speak to her at first. Some of her words were just sounds, like water falling into a cup, smooth and steady and cool, but usually I knew what she meant by listening, and trying to feel where her mind was.

"I will teach you," she said on that first day. When I had finished brushing her hair she fastened it back with a blue elastic band and smiled at me. "It will give me something to do. We will learn things together."

She went to another room and brought back a book with some pictures. When she turned the pages the paper crackled as if the book hadn't been opened for a long, long time and the smell of it was old. "Look," she said, "your people."

I didn't see any of *my* people. Nobody that I knew, but there were pictures of people very like them and there was one who might even have been old Kamha, although with far fewer wrinkles. Also they weren't wearing proper clothes, but only bits of leather.

"You come from a proud race, Be," Min said. "A proud, dying race. There are hardly any of you left."

Min's eyes were so serious when she said that that I didn't think I should tell her that there were really quite a lot of us, and many new babies and other children, so I couldn't see how we could be disappearing like she seemed to think we were.

"Once your people lived everywhere in Africa."

Min waved her arm so that I had to look where she was pointing, and there was the gray, dusty road leading to Africa.

"Great artists," Min said, and she turned the musty pages of the old book until there was a picture of a cave with some scratchy animals painted on the rock. "Great hunters." Which I knew was true. "In the past," Min went on.

I wanted to tell her then about how Hau shot the wildebeest when he was on the way to the meeting of the Farmers' Cooperative and then came back later, after the meeting with the government people, and asked for the truck to be stopped, and tracked that wildebeest to the place where it died. I *wanted* to tell her that, but I felt somehow that wasn't what she wanted to hear.

"Yes. A dying race." Min sighed then as if she felt very sorry for us. "But I will teach you. Yes. That's what I'll do."

Most days after that, when she was well enough, Min taught me something. Some of the things were very useful, like English words that I didn't know yet. Some of the things were rather strange. We had to do embroidery, and Min brought colored threads and a needle that was too small and taught me to make flowers on a white cloth. I didn't really see that this was going to be a useful thing to know, but it pleased Min and that meant that it pleased me.

Min brought some new books from the town. They were very shiny and the pages were white and smooth and new. I liked them much better than the old book about Bushmen and they smelled better too, but sometimes Min brought the old one out again and we looked at the pictures of the people I didn't know, and felt sad about the dying race.

Kleinbaas was a bit suspicious at first. "Kid ought to be working. Doing something useful," he said.

Min got quite angry then and her very pale face went pink. "She's only a child, Koos!"

That was the only time I heard that Kleinbaas was called Koos. It sounded like a good name for him.

"She's only . . . How old are you, Be?"

Then I felt ashamed, because I didn't know and I looked at the carpet instead of at Min.

"You see! She can't even *count* yet!"

Kleinbaas laughed then, as if Min had said something very funny, but he didn't stop my having lessons and there was still time for me to help Aia when she got tired, and help with the other work Kleinbaas wanted me to do with the calves and in the vegetable garden.

I think I was happy during that first time on Ontevrede. Not happy like I was in the village when I was very small, but not unhappy. Sometimes the days were good.

It's very still, here under the thorn tree. All around me is stillness and there are no voices for many days' walk. When I am remembering, my mind doesn't think about the poison. My head hurts. Is it beginning to work?

I have decided that I will go now to gather food from the veld, even though I'm not hungry. It will make my mind still again, to look for the berries and the places where the bulbs are, under the ground. I have my digging stick and I will dig them up, just like Aia taught me when I was small. Then I'll make a fire and I'll roast the bulbs until they're soft, and eat them before I go to sleep.

Far over there, at the farthest place my eyes can see,

25

is a baobab tree. I think I'll walk there before I make my fire, and then lie under it, with its great black branches stretching over my head. And look at the stars.

3

Here under the baobab is a good place. The birds were still flying when I came and it was the end of the light. I started my fire and I've put my tin cooking pot on it with some tsama melon and a little water from one of my ostrich shells. The smell of the soup is drifting past my nose, but I'm not really hungry. There doesn't seem much point in eating. Not now.

When I lie back on the kudu skin that Aia made for me, my eyes look up past the huge, wrinkled trunk of the tree and on through the massive branches. Far above them is the sky, black and dark tonight, with no moon and no bright, shining stars. My mind is sad, as if the end of something is near. There were so many things that I could have done differently. So many thoughts that I should have had, and didn't, until it was too late.

There are things that maybe I only came to understand with my growing. Or maybe I was just too stupid to see what was happening in front of my eyes.

◈ It was hard for Aia and Grandfather, that time. For me every day had some sunshine in it. For them, I see now, it was a gray, bleak time with work and loneliness, and other things.

Day came after day. In the mornings Aia worked in the house and in the afternoons she helped on the farm. There was always work for her to do. At night sometimes she even had to go and do mending for Kleinbaas. Min couldn't do it, she said, because she wasn't very good at sewing. I used to be angry when Aia took the big basket of torn shirts and socks with holes in them.

"It's not *fair!*" I said. "You should be resting now, not working still." But Aia just smiled and carried the basket over to the big kitchen, where, she said, there was better light by which to sew.

Her smile had changed. It wasn't like the smile she had when she lived in our own place. It was tired and a little sad. Sometimes Aia's smile made me afraid but I didn't know why.

Grandfather was happy that we had come, but he was not happy in his heart. Once I asked Aia why he stayed with Kleinbaas. She thought for a long time before she answered.

"I can't say, Be," she said at last. "My father has been here for a long time. He is used to this place."

"But he could go home! To his own place, and be with our people!"

Aia looked sad then. "Maybe he has been too long with Mr. Coetzee. They know each other. Maybe he has been so long here that it would be hard for him to go back."

I could think of nothing about Mr. Coetzee that would make *me* stay. Also, surely Grandfather could see that Aia wasn't happy either? She should be married again, with more small children, not working and working at a place where she didn't belong. There were many puzzles in this new life of ours, and this was not the smallest one to me.

Aia took some of the work from Grandfather. She led the milk cows out to the veld in the morning, before she went to the house, and brought them in again at night, and I helped. It was good to be with the cows, feeling their soft warmth all around and smelling their smell. We could feel that Kleinbaas watched us, very carefully at first, to make sure that we did it right. He didn't say anything, but he didn't get angry either, so we knew that it was all right.

It took Aia a lot longer to understand the things she had to do in the house. Everything was new to her and sometimes Min didn't understand this. I tried to explain, I tried to tell Min how we had lived before, but there seems to be something inside people that stops them from listening—that stops them from making pictures in their minds of things they haven't seen.

Maybe Min wanted to think we were like the people in the old book with the pictures. Maybe she thought that my people hadn't changed at all in a hundred years. But she didn't think what that would mean to somebody like Aia, who had never been inside a proper house before.

Once I wrote a story for Min, so she could see the words written down, black on white.

Our home is in a village called /Aotcha, in Nyae Nyae, which is a part of Eastern Bushmanland. It is a long way to walk—even when sometimes you have help from a donkey cart driver and a man with a truck.

29

My father died when I was too small to remember, so Aia and I lived alone in a small shelter. Aia often went to gather food from the veld and when there was meat from hunting we had our share, just like the other people in the village who had fathers and husbands.

Aia often worked in the gardens which we had started to grow, carrying the water in a square tin to water the mealies and melons and beans.

She made beads from ostrich shells to sell to the rich tourists who came from Windhoek, and small leather bags with bright beads sewn onto them.

We shared what we had and the other people shared what they had. Except in the dry time, during the winter, we always had enough to eat and sometimes a little money to buy extra things that we needed.

But there were no bright, shining things in our shelter, no glass windows and polished floors, no cups and saucers made of thin stuff that breaks, no carpets with bright blue and red. Aia doesn't know these things.

Instead we had soft grass to sleep on and the floor was of gray dust. We had tin cups to drink out of and no silver forks or knives with which to eat.

It made me sad to write that story for Min, to remember our place, and I had to stop before I was really finished. But Min was pleased when she read it. She got out the red pen she had bought (because she said she wanted to be like a proper teacher) and made a big red star beside my story and said that she was very pleased with my progress. But I don't think she listened to what my story was trying to say to her. Min only listened to the things that were inside her.

Min was like a sky spirit anchored to the world by a thin thread. She was good and gentle and caring, but she was not quite real. Some afternoons I went to the farmhouse for my lesson and wondered if she would still be there, or if she might have floated away somewhere in the night, like a wandering star or a quiet wind. Sometimes she had.

"Mrs. Coetzee isn't well," Kleinbaas would say angrily. "Go away. Stop bothering her."

But I think Kleinbaas could see that Min enjoyed our times together. He didn't like it, but he had to allow it, and the times when he grumbled darkly about putting me to work on the farm, Min would smile and say I was still too young.

"Stupid Bushmen!" Kleinbaas often said. "Educating one of them is a waste of time. She'll just disappear back to her hut in the veld one day and all your hard work will be a waste of time. You'll never get anything back out of her. Waste of time!" And Kleinbaas would stamp off to go and mend the wind pump that was always breaking down, or to watch the Hereros dipping the cattle. Min just smiled.

But there came a time when Min was less and less well. More days than not I would go to the back door and be angrily turned away by Kleinbaas. The fear began to grow in me that Min would die, that my friend would no longer be there.

I worked harder. I studied late into the night with the fluttering candle flame lighting my books. Aia worried about me when she came in and found me like that.

"It's too late, Be! Come to sleep."

"I just want to finish this chapter."

31

Min got the books from the library in Gobabis when she went there sometimes with Kleinbaas for the shopping—when she was well enough to go. These books all had colored pictures, not like the black-and-white ones in the old book. She also got cards for me so I could have three books a month, saying that I was her cousin's child and she would be responsible.

In the beginning they were books with big pictures and not many words. Later they had no pictures and many words that were difficult, but I wanted to learn. I wanted to read. Reading, for me, was like looking down an ant-bear tunnel and seeing another world inside it, a world that was better than the one I had.

"Do they really have villages that are so big?"

Min laughed and looked over my shoulder at the picture in the book. "That, Be, is London, where I went once when I was a student, long before I married Mr. Coetzee, and yes, it is so big, and no, it isn't a village, but a city."

I looked at that picture for a long time. It was taken from somewhere high up so that you could see the roads and the high buildings with glass walls and the broad river winding through. They must have a very big rainy season there, I thought.

There were so many things that Min knew, so many things that I didn't know. I think she liked sharing with me, teaching me. I think it filled the emptiness of her afternoons—and maybe more than that. We would sit at the small table in Min's room with the books from the library and the pencils and exercise books, and I learned.

Then I would brush Min's hair for her—she always

liked that. Sometimes she would close her eyes and we would be quiet except for the smooth sound of the brush through her long, pale hair. And then, when I had finished brushing, Min would let me hold one of her dolls, very carefully, and she would tell me a story she had made up in her own head.

I loved Min. And she helped me not to miss Aia so much.

All the while the time was passing, and around me were dark things that I didn't see.

I think the end of the good time for me at Ontevrede was after the man came from the American newspaper. I remember that day very clearly. Min had a headache and Kleinbaas had gone to Gobabis to buy diesel, taking Aia with him to get the things we needed for the house. I was sitting with my back against the wall of the cow shed, working on my lesson for the next time that Min was well.

It was very quiet by the cow shed. Everyone had gone. I felt . . . abandoned. Like . . . There was a day when we were still at /Aotcha. We were out gathering and one of the small ones, Debe, was somehow left behind. Everyone went in different directions to look for him—I did too—and then I heard they had found him. I heard their laughing and Nai, who was Debe's mother, pretending to be angry with him, and the other women—Aia too—telling her not to beat him too hard. Debe cried again and then they all laughed, because nobody was going to beat him anyway. They just wanted to make him remember so that he wouldn't do it again.

I was maybe eight years old at that time, old enough

for the women not to have to worry about me all the time and look for me. I waited. Nobody called out, not even Aia, and their voices went away, becoming smaller, until there was no sound at all except the shiver of the sand as the ants moved across it and it ran down in little rivers.

That was the first time I had ever been alone, but differently. I was truly alone now. Aia had gone from me again, but this time in some strange way that I didn't understand.

Sitting at Ontevrede that afternoon, feeling the rough stone of the cow shed wall through my T-shirt, and the new spring sun on my legs, I tried to forget.

It had been a cold winter with frost every night for weeks. Minus-seven, Kleinbaas said it was one night. I heard him telling Grandfather.

"Minus bloody seven!" Kleinbaas said. "Bloody climate! Get the bloody stuff through the heat and the drought and bloody frost comes and kills it!"

Kleinbaas was talking about the vegetable garden and he was especially angry because the gray loerie birds had just eaten the last of the lettuces. The ones that had not been killed by the minus-seven because they'd been covered with sacks.

"Bloody birds! Eat the money right out of your pocket, they would. Next thing the bloody cows will get sick!" Then he stamped off to his truck to load the diesel cans.

The reporter came about half an hour after that. He had strange clothes and a funny way of talking.

"Say, is Mis Koot-zeee in?" he asked Moses, who was passing with a load of cow muck in a wheelbarrow.

34

Moses just looked at the man. Moses isn't stupid, but sometimes he likes to act it. The man was kind of edging away from Moses's wheelbarrow, so Moses moved it a bit nearer.

"What?" Moses said.

"Miz Koot-zeee. Is she around?"

The man edged away for a bit of fresh air. Moses pushed the wheelbarrow so it was practically under his nose.

"What?"

I felt sorry for the man then. Moses, I knew, could play that game all day if he felt like it.

"Mrs. Coetzee isn't well," I told the man. "She's lying down."

I saw then that he was really quite young. His face went all kind of crumpled with disappointment.

"Oh, hang!" he said. "I've come all the way out from Gobabis to see her. I got her name from somebody who knew her at college. He said she'd be a good contact."

And then he seemed really to see me for the first time.

"Say! Are you a real, live Bushman?"

"Yes," I told him. "I am a Ju/'hoan of Eastern Bushmanland and I am also real."

Well, after that it was as if I'd given him a present. He got out a black notebook and a green pen and started writing down stuff.

"Can you tell me what you think the new government is going to do about Bushmanland after the election?"

I told him I didn't know.

"What do you think about the men who were in the

35

war—up north—the Bushmen Battalion? What's going to happen to them?"

I told him that only one man from our village had been in the army and he had come back with a portable tape recorder. That was all I knew about that. Also he had learned to drink while he was in the army, but luckily, when he came home, he soon ran out of money, so *that* didn't last long.

The man wrote everything down. We went and sat on the low wall that runs around the empty vegetable patch. It was nice having somebody actually listen to what I was trying to say.

"How much do they pay you for working here?"

I told him they didn't pay me anything, but that Min gave me lessons instead. That really made him excited and his pen fairly flew across the page.

In the back of my mind was a small picture of Kleinbaas and what he would think if he could hear me saying those words. And then I thought, Well, it's true, isn't it? And what did it matter anyway?

"And what kind of food do they give you?"

Well, I told him, before the gray loerie birds and the frost, and before the heat and the drought, we used to get vegetables, but lately we had mostly mealie porridge, and meat once a week. And that was true too, although I didn't tell him that Kleinbaas wasn't eating meat much either, just now, and that quite often Aia had to cook them tinned fish and potatoes and stuff like that instead of beef or mutton.

"And how often do you get to go home? For holidays?"

Holidays were something I had read about in the readers Min got when I was first learning English. The ones where John and Mary went to the sea. But I'd never been to the sea and I'd never been home since Aia and I left there to come and help Grandfather. He wrote that down as well.

Then he asked if he could see where Aia and I lived. Well, I didn't mind showing him. Aia and I had fixed it up really nicely, although Min never had remembered about the curtains. We'd collected the wooden boxes that Kleinbaas used to send the eggs in, before the hens died of Newcastle disease. We'd scrubbed the boxes and put our things neatly inside. We had more things now, because Min had given Aia overalls to wear when she worked in the house. I had a pair of sandals and some pink socks she had bought me once in town, and there were my schoolbooks, with a special chicken box all of their own. Kleinbaas had complained about the shoes and socks, but Min told him it was a disgrace to see a child walking barefoot in this day and age. I didn't wear them very often, only when it was really cold. My toes liked the feel of the dust in between them.

When he saw our room I thought the man must have really been impressed because he took out a camera and made flashes with it, and all the time he was muttering, "Beautiful! Beautiful!" and then he made a lot more notes.

At the back of my mind I was getting a bit scared that Kleinbaas would come back then. I didn't think Kleinbaas would like my talking to strange people when he wasn't there. I also didn't think that Kleinbaas would like to know that somebody was taking pictures of his farm just then. It wasn't looking at its best after the long winter and the frost. It would

37

have been much better to take the pictures when the rains had come, and the veld was green and beautiful.

So I was quite glad when the man shook my hand and got back into his car. He'd only been there an hour, and nobody knew he'd come—except Moses, and he didn't count.

4

Min was sick again the next day and Kleinbaas, as usual, was angry.

"Just get *out* of here!" he shouted when I knocked on the back door. "Bloody Bushmen. Give them a finger and they want your whole hand! It's time I found some real work for you to do."

But that day I didn't run away to the cow shed like I normally did when Kleinbaas shouted at me. I stayed near the door. I wanted to see if I could do anything to help Min.

So that was how I found out the terrible thing.

Once, in our village, a message came for one of our old people. It came with the truck of the magistrate and a black man brought it. His face was sorrowful and a little afraid and in his hand was a blue paper.

"Where is Gishay?" he said quickly.

"Gishay is in the veld, hunting," he was told.

His face changed then, as if he was glad he might be able to escape before Gishay came back. "Is there anyone here who can read?" His eyes looked at our huts and shelters and I could see that he didn't expect there would be.

Xama nodded once. "In which language?" she asked.

The man looked surprised. "I think it's in English."

Xama nodded again, with great dignity. "There are some who can read English and some who can read Afrikaans. Also there is one who learned to speak and read German at the school in Windhoek and a few who speak Damara and Herero."

The man looked as though he didn't quite believe that, although I knew it was true. But if he believed, it meant that he could escape and he would not have to tell Gishay. So he gave the paper to Xama and then we watched the dust from his truck, and the wheels spinning in it.

Xama sighed. "This paper will not bring happiness."

It didn't.

Never before had I seen real sorrow. Always the people were smiling and their arms were soft and brown and loving. "Come, Be," they would say, and there would be happiness.

But today was the news of the death of Gishay's son and the people turned inside themselves and had no place there for anything but grief. I looked into Gishay's eyes later that night, after he had read the paper, and I saw, for the first time, what grief was.

Min's eyes, on that morning when I waited at the door, were the same.

I think this is what makes people old, this sorrow, this pain that is too much. Before the bad time at Ontevrede I was young. After, I was old.

Aia had gone to help in the lands that day, and I went to the farmhouse on my own. I knew Kleinbaas had gone too because I'd seen his truck and the thin line of whitish dust that spread behind it as he went.

Min was in the room with the sunshine-yellow curtains. I went there because when I stood near the door at the back of the house I could hear her crying. Min was my friend and I wanted to help her, but the door was locked and I couldn't get in.

Her crying was tearing at my heart, so I did something that I knew would make Kleinbaas very angry if he found out. I got the ladder that stands near the water windmill and I propped it up against the wall of the house. The windows on that side are very high and I was frightened when the ladder shook. I thought I was going to fall off, but I could still hear Min crying and that made me climb to the top.

There was a little space between the curtains and I looked inside.

Min was kneeling beside the bed. Her beautiful yellow hair was everywhere, all mixed up over her face, and her eyes were almost shut from crying. She rocked and rocked on her knees and banged her head against the end of the bed. When she spoke her words were wild and meaningless.

There was a crack at the top of the window frame, so I pushed and pulled at it with my fingers until the window began to slide up. The ladder was shaking like a tree in the wind, but I didn't care. I just wanted to get inside and help Min.

In the end I almost fell into the room, making such a terrible noise that I thought Kleinbaas might even hear me all that way away, but he didn't come. He didn't hear. And neither did Min.

She turned her face toward me, but she didn't see me, not then or later. She just kept speaking the words, over and over again, that made no sense at all. The sorrow was in her face, the sorrow like Gishay's when the news came about his son, and I saw then that Min was quite, quite mad.

I don't remember a lot more about that day. I tried to help Min. I washed her face with a cool cloth. Kleinbaas had left water in a glass jug but she had broken that. The key to the locked door was missing, so I had to climb out of the window to get some water from the rain barrel. I brought the small brush as well, to sweep up the glass. It worried me that Kleinbaas would know I had been there if he saw that the jug was gone, but it worried me more that Min would cut herself.

I tried to brush Min's hair because often she liked me to do that, but she pulled away from me and pulled at her hair as well, crying all the time in that soft, hopeless way as she rocked and rocked, backward and forward, backward and forward. And I was crying, too.

Toward late afternoon she seemed to be calmer and I managed to get her up onto the bed. She lay there quite still and she had stopped crying, but her eyes were wild and she worked and worked her hands until I thought the bones might crack.

I was very afraid. What would Kleinbaas do if he found me there?

I wiped her face again with the cool cloth and tried once more to brush her hair. This time it seemed to soothe her a little. Gradually her hands stopped twisting. After a time she fell into a deep sleep.

I sat with her as long as I dared, but I knew the people would be coming in from the lands soon. It was starting to get dark. Aia would be looking for me to help with the milk cows. And Kleinbaas . . .

Very quietly I started to creep out of the window again, but I must have made some sound because Min spoke to me from the bed. Her voice was dry and empty and unbelievably tired.

"Thank you, Be," she said. "So now you also know."

I couldn't think what to say. Min leaned up on one arm and I knew she was looking at me at last, although it was too dark to see her eyes.

"Sometimes it is . . . very bad . . . like today. Sometimes it is better. Sometimes there are whole months with nothing. I never know when . . . when it will come."

My voice was only a whisper. "Min, I'm so sorry."

Min sighed. "It's getting worse." Her voice, when she said that, was flat and empty and dead.

Then my heart knew that there were no words that I could say. Quietly I slipped out through the window and pulled it down behind me. When I looked up, from the bottom of the ladder, there was just the dark square of glass and no sound coming from inside.

Aia was back when I got to the cow shed and had already started with the cows. She looked at me strangely when I came in.

"Is something wrong, Be?"

But I couldn't tell her. Not even Aia. It was Min's well-kept secret—Min's and the Kleinbaas's. I had gone where I was not supposed to go, and the knowledge of what I had found was hard to bear.

All that evening I thought and thought about what I could do—about what I should do. I remembered things that had been said in the past—and things that had not been said—and I wondered how I could have been so stupid for so long, and so uncaring.

43

At last, when Aia went to take Grandfather his food, I walked across the darkened farmyard to the back door. I didn't care if Kleinbaas was angry. I had to be brave enough for that. I would tell him that I knew about Min's sickness and I wanted to help her, as she had helped me, and look after her when she needed me. And I was going to do it now, before I had time to be afraid again.

But when I came to the door it was open, as if Kleinbaas had forgotten to shut it. Kleinbaas was sitting at the kitchen table with his head in his hands, and the pool of tears shone yellow in the light from the lamp on the dresser.

I went away and left him alone.

Ontevrede was full of secrets. Because my eyes had been opened to one . . . I began to look. And I began to see. Like lions in the night, the secrets ringed us with hate and fear.

"Why do you stay here, Grandfather?" I can hear my voice, challenging him. It was morning, early morning, and there were white clouds in the frosty air where the cows breathed through their soft noses.

Grandfather didn't answer for a while. He just went on forking the feed into the feed troughs. When he did speak, I thought at first that it was about something else.

"I was young when they brought me here," he said at last. "It was the year after they had their great fighting in the far lands, the big war between the Germans and the English, and there were changes on the farms. New things."

For a while he was silent again, concentrating on his work. "Do you know how I came to Ontevrede?"

"No, Grandfather."

"I came on the back of a two-ton truck, with two other Bushmen boys, and our hands and feet were tied with rope so that we could not escape."

I must have shown in my face that I didn't know whether to believe this.

"Oh yes, it's true." Grandfather's voice wasn't bitter. He was just saying something that was true, something that had happened. "They came for us in the late night when we were sleeping beside our fire. We were tired that night, tired from a long hunt, and we were full with the meat of the eland we had killed with our arrows." Grandfather smiled a little. "It was good, that meat. I remember it well because it was the last I had for a long time. Two days we had tracked the eland, waiting for it to fall so that we could finish it off with our spears. It was Toma's first kill and we were wild with the excitement of it.

"It was too late to carry home the meat to our families, so we cooked the soft inside meat for ourselves and cut up the carcass ready to carry home the next day. Then we lay down to rest. We were sleeping as only the young can sleep and our ears were closed to the sound of the engine, so that when the father of Kleinbaas came with his men, it was too late for us to run away."

Grandfather went calmly on with his work.

The horror of it sprang up inside me like anger. "But how could they do this?"

"It was the custom. It was not an unknown thing for the farmers to come with their horses and trucks and guns and carry off our young people to work for them."

This had not been written in the old book with the black-and-white photographs that Min had.

"But didn't you run away?"

Grandfather stopped working then. He put down the fork and rested his back against the shed door, looking out toward the edge of Ontevrede, where the boundary fence was.

"Yes. We ran away. Toma was shot."

"Shot? Shot . . . dead?"

"Dead."

For a moment we were both silent. "And your other friend? The other hunter who was taken with you?"

"Dead too. Only three months after we were taken." Grandfather sighed. "He just couldn't bear to go on living, so he didn't."

"But you must have gone home. You can't have stayed here all your life, just working on Ontevrede!" I remember the anger I felt that Grandfather had lived nothing else than this.

"I went back. Once." His eyes when he said that were sad. Sadder than I had ever seen them, sadder even than when he had spoken of Toma's death.

"I went back when Oubaas, Kleinbaas's father, died. I went to /Aotcha, which was my n!ore, the place where I belonged, the place of my fathers. I went there and I found my people had gone to a new place, which was not our n!ore, a place where the white people said we must come, because they wanted to help us. They said they would build houses for us and there would be jobs and we would be . . . civilized. Yes, *civilized* was the word they used. For us it was a place of death."

Inside me was a cold feeling brought there by Grandfather's words. It seemed that now that he had begun to speak, the words wouldn't stop, but just kept on coming—and each of them was worse than the last.

"I came to the location where they had built the houses for my people. My father was long dead, killed when he fell from a great baobab tree while he was hunting for honey. But my mother was there and one of my brothers and his wife. They were glad to see me, glad to have the money I had saved, glad to eat the food I had brought. That night, they said, we must celebrate. We must make party, they said. One of my brothers went to the bottle store in the village and bought strong drink and they drank it, all of them, even my mother, until they fell down drunk and I had to pull her hair away from the fire or she would have burned in it."

These words were like ice to hear, cold and thin and dead.

"I stayed for a time—a year maybe. I married your grandmother and I got a job cutting fencing posts for the government. We found a hut in the location where the people had left and there was room for us to stay. I waited until our child was born—your mother—and then I could not stay there any longer."

Grandfather's voice was very quiet, as if he couldn't even bear to remember that time. "That place was death and sickness to me. It was the coughing of the old people and the crying of the babies who had no proper food. It was the young men lying drunk in the street and the fighting when the drink was in them. It was cutting and cutting at posts for the government and no time for me to be myself! No time for me to be a man among my people."

He sighed, a deep sigh that shook him so that he coughed again. "In my father's time it was not so. Then we had our land, our n!ore, our place. We had our water holes and our animals. We knew how to hunt so that everything was not dead when we had done with hunting. We knew how to live so that everything was not destroyed and even the small tortoises in our veld were safe. Yes."

For a long time we both were silent. When Grandfather started to speak again, his voice was so soft that I could hardly hear it, soft like the small wind that blows before the sun comes back in the morning, soft like the moving of the stars.

"I could not stay in that place. So I came back to the only place I had. I came home to Ontevrede."

I stayed with Grandfather all morning after that, helping him with the milking and with the weeding in the vegetable garden. He had told me something to make me think, something terrible. But he hadn't told me everything.

Something strange happened today. My eyes hurt in the bright light, but I thought I saw someone moving toward me across the pan. I thought . . . After a while I thought it was Aia, although I knew that was impossible. Her shape wavered and shook in the hot shimmering air. I think I called out to her, but the shape disappeared and left behind only the tears on my cheeks to remember it by. I felt very lonely then. So lonely that I wished I was already dead.

Why is it taking so long?

◈ Once Min brought a book from the library. It was a story about a girl who was searching for her sister. It was so exciting that I could hardly wait for the end to find out what happened. And then Kleinbaas came in.

"Is that kid here again?" he shouted at Min. "She wastes too much time with this stupid learning—and so do you!" Kleinbaas threw the book across the room so that it landed on the floor, facedown on the carpet. "Get out of here!" he said to me, and then he sat down quickly with the tired look he often had. "God, this farm is going to drive me to death," he said to Min.

Something was wrong again, on Ontevrede. As it often was. Min quickly showed that I should go. As I left, I heard her voice, soft and soothing, talking to Kleinbaas.

The next day, she forgot that I hadn't finished the book, and she took it back to the library in Gobabis, so that I never did discover whether the girl found her sister.

I was like that again after I spoke to Grandfather—wanting to know the end. I had found some beginnings, now I wanted to know how all of them fitted together. Grandfather and Kleinbaas and Min and Aia all had threads drawing their lives together—and mine too. I wanted to know what they were. I wanted to know.

"What was it like when you were young?" I asked Aia. Aia was ironing, so she could talk and work at the same time. The iron went "thump, thump" on the shirts while she thought in silence before she answered.

"It was different to what you remember of your childhood." She smiled. "What do you remember best, Be?" But I wasn't going to be put off that easily.

Aia sighed. "I was born at the location in Tsumkwe, where my mother lived. Do you remember Tsumkwe?"

Yes, I remembered it. I had been there once, on the truck from our village. This was the place Grandfather had spoken of, the place of death to his people.

"Tsumkwe was . . . was not like /Aotcha, where I took you when you were a baby. Tsumkwe was . . ." The words seemed to be difficult for Aia to find. "It was . . . a hard place."

Aia swept the iron over a tablecloth without really seeing it. "It was a place where our people had tried something that didn't work. They tried to leave the veld where we had always lived in order to find jobs, to work for money, to live in the houses the government built for us. But it didn't work."

I remembered the old book of Min's, the pictures of Bushmen sitting around fires, wearing bits of leather, going without water. There were no windmills to pump for them, no warm clothes, no tins of milk powder for the babies. Surely that wasn't better?

Aia seemed to know what I was thinking. She put down the iron and looked right at me for the first time. "Remember, Be, that you are a Ju/'hoan. I think, maybe, that some of us forgot that for a time. Now we are remembering."

"Is that why you went back to /Aotcha?"

"That, and other reasons." Aia's lips were pulled in a tight, straight line. She looked angry. The iron was thumping again, this time on one of Min's skirts.

And then Aia looked at me again and her face softened.

"Oh, Be, how can I tell you? How can anyone tell another person what it was like?"

She put the iron down carefully and stopped for a moment to think before she went on.

"They talked, the old people. Bushmen always talk, they say, around their fires and over their tobacco, they talk and talk of things past and things now.

"My mother used to tell me what it was like before they came to Tsumkwe. I used to wonder, even then, how much of it was true and how much was a memory grown better with time.

51

"I would look around me at the dirt and the litter and the people sitting doing nothing. At night I would listen to the sounds—people singing and then people fighting after the drink had come to them. I would look at their faces—at the hope that had gone from them—and I would wish and wish for the old times.

"And then your father came."

Aia had never before spoken of my father and somehow I had always known I should not ask.

"There was a day. It was the time of the rains and the sky was green-gray with water. Good rains, we had, that year. We lived and we lived. We waited and we waited and the time was slow and still. Wait, it said, wait. But inside me I did not want to wait. Inside I was tired of being who I was, a child of no n!ore, a child of the squatter camp that was Tsumkwe. Inside were changes and things in my mind that said *now*. Now you are woman. And I could not wait."

Aia stopped. Her eyes were in another time. They looked at another place.

"Yes. It was the time your father came. You will know too, Be. When it happens to you, you also will know."

She was quiet for so long this time that I gave a little jump of surprise when she spoke again.

"Eh-hey!" Aia said, and her eyes held a sparkle I had not seen there before.

"But he was fine, your father! His skin was pale and smooth like yours and his smile was like yours, too. And his fingers, when he touched me, were cool and dry. I thought I felt the pulse of his heart in them, yes I did.

"I remember the smell of the honey he brought me

and the smell of the bush where we lay. I remember the sound of the rain falling and falling about us and his laughter, low and cool, like the soft rain. I remember his laughter."

For a time we were both silent.

"Then why did you leave?" I said at last. "Why did you go back to /Aotcha?" I knew that Aia didn't want to speak of these things, but I had to know.

Aia's eyes were angry again, although not with me. She took up a green shirt from the basket beside her and held the iron once more, like a weapon, like a beating stone.

"After your father died—" She stopped and started again. "After your father was killed in a fight over another woman, I took you—you were about a year old— and I went to where my uncle was trying to begin again at /Aotcha, and I went back to the way we had been. We took with us the things we had learned in our years at the village: how to plant vegetables and how to keep cattle in a kraal at night to protect them against the lions, and we went back."

"But why—"

Aia stopped my question angrily. "Because I was afraid. I brought you here, to Ontevrede, because I was afraid!"

She glared at me, daring me to ask any more questions. "Now will you stop! Stop pushing into places you do not need to be!"

Then we both noticed, for the first time, the black smoke rising from under the iron. Aia lifted it and her face was tired again and no longer angry. "Now look what you've made me do! I think you had better see to the calves."

I wish . . . I wish I could die now, before I have to re-member the next bit. It wasn't my fault! It really wasn't all my fault—but some of it was. And there is Khu, who comes into the story right now, and I don't want to remember him. I don't think I can bear to re-member him. But it has come to my mind that maybe the poison is waiting for me to remember everything. Maybe then I will be clean of the things that hap-pened last summer at Ontevrede. Maybe then I can rest.

Khu was like the taste of cool water. Khu was like the scent of the first rain on the veld, like the shape of the sun when it has just appeared over the edge of the world, smooth and round and handsome.

I loved him.

He came late one afternoon when we had just fin-ished with the cattle in the shed and I was on my way back to the house to see if Min needed any vegetables brought from the garden.

Such an ordinary day. Such ordinary things.

"Good day. I'm looking for Dam. I was told I would find him on this farm."

And my heart, which had been doing ordinary things, just like me, stopped beating for a moment, and when it started again . . . it was his.

He smiled. "I'm sorry. Did I frighten you? I thought you had seen me coming." He waved his hand to where a red four-wheel drive was parked. "I have come from /Aotcha to bring this man Dam a message. Do you know him?"

I think I must have said something, but I don't remember what it was. I do remember that somehow we were inside the cow shed and Grandfather was there, and the two of them were talking, and my ears were listening, although the rest of me was floating about somewhere else.

"I bring a message. From your brother's wife," Khu said when they had finished greeting each other and Khu had explained where he had come from. "She says that they need you to come back. They want you."

Grandfather was very still.

"This is a time when new things are beginning. The old government will soon be gone and we need wise voices to speak to the new government that will come after the elections."

We knew about the elections. Men had come in trucks with red and blue and white flags and given us T-shirts, and other men had come with red and green and blue flags and given us other T-shirts. Aia said we must be very careful. Aia said she didn't trust new things. With the old government we knew what to expect, even if it was bad. Who knew what would happen when they went?

Khu was speaking again. "Our people have been scattered and thrown all over this country. We want you to come home, to your n!ore. We all want this. I have been sent to bring this message to all our people on the farms of the Gobabis District."

Grandfather still did not speak.

"Things have changed in Bushmanland. Our people have united so that there are voices to speak for us. We have had meetings—many meetings—and we know what we want to say about our land, our n!ores, and our lives. We have sent our young people to school to learn for us and our old people have even been to Windhoek to speak for us."

Grandfather cleared his throat as if he wanted to speak, but still no words came.

"Please. We need all our people. All their knowledge, because we are beginning with new things—with things we have never done before, things you have learned here on the farm. We need you. There is a place for you."

And then Grandfather spoke. "I can't," he said. That was all he would say.

I was angry. Mostly I was angry because I thought Khu would go and I didn't want that to happen.

"Think about it," Khu said. Then he turned to me. "Is there a place where I can sleep for the night?" He looked around the cow shed. "In here would do, if the farmer wouldn't mind."

Kleinbaas spoke suddenly from behind us. "The farmer does mind! Who gave you permission to come on my land?"

Khu turned easily, not like Grandfather would have, or Aia, or me, but as if he was ready for Kleinbaas, as if he knew him, as if he was equal. "I'm sorry. I understood that this man has given you long and loyal service. I thought you would understand that his people wish to speak to him at this time."

Kleinbaas grunted. "Dam belongs here. You don't. Now clear off before I fetch my shotgun."

There was a moment when Khu just stared at Kleinbaas. Then he shrugged. "All right. I understand." He looked calmly around the cow shed and I saw it for the first time through someone else's eyes: the worn leather and the rusty hinges; the tired old cows and their battered stalls. I saw for the first time that Ontevrede was not rich.

"I'll come back when I have been to the others," Khu said to Grandfather. "You have your rights, you know, and so does this girl." He nodded to me. "Maybe she would like to be part of a new life, even if you have your . . . commitments."

He nodded toward Kleinbaas and smiled at me.

He did smile. He did.

"Good-bye."

Grandfather and Kleinbaas and I were still standing as if we had been caught in the minus-seven when we heard the sound of the red four-wheel drive retreating down the dusty farm road.

It was nearly dark when Khu came back. Aia was working in the kitchen—mending again, she said—and I was angry. Why did my mother have to do these things? Why could we not be like the people in the books Min brought me? Why?

Aia told me to go. Aia said I should sleep because I was tired from too much working with my books. I was angry about that, too.

Khu's voice came to me while I was walking back to our room.

"Be? Is that your name?"

He was in the shadow beside the cow shed, but now he stepped out so that the faint light from the kitchen window revealed him to me. "Can I talk to you?"

I must have looked behind me nervously, I think, because Khu laughed softly.

"He doesn't *own* you, you know!"

"No."

"We need to talk, Be."

"Yes."

We walked down the road toward the gate. There wasn't anywhere else to walk.

"Do you know about the elections, Be? About the changes?"

I nodded, and then remembered that he couldn't see in the dark. "Yes. Min told me. The farmer's wife."

"Things are going to change, Be. You may be too young to vote, but they will change for you, too."

And then he told me about the speeches and the riding from place to place in the four-wheel drive. He talked and his eyes shone in the faint light from the moon, which appeared from behind the mealie field.

"The people gather together—they come from everywhere, Be, and they sit and they listen and then they ask—and I can see hope in their eyes! Our elder people, our old men and women, and some of the young ones, too. They speak and the people listen and now they are ready to register and to vote and then we too will have a voice in this new nation that will be Namibia!"

And then he stopped walking. My feet stopped, too. He took my hand as if that too was part of the new things.

"You are very beautiful, Be."

Nobody had ever told me that before. I just looked at Khu, and looked.

And then we were beside the gate where the red four-wheel drive was standing. Khu let go of my hand then, but he touched my cheek lightly with his fingers before he jumped up into the cab.

"I will see you again, Be. I will see you again."

I don't know if he heard my whispered good-bye in the roar of sound from the truck.

Now the secrets weren't like lions in the dark behind us. They were like bubbles in a pot of mealie porridge, and they were right in our midst.

Times, Aia said, were changing. It was the elections that were changing the times—fast. New words came to us. Resolution 435 came to us, when all the countries met in New York and made a decision that meant that Namibia should belong to its own people—Nama, Ovambo, Damara, Hai//om, English, Basters—even Ju/wasi. All. All would be Namibians and all would have a voice.

"Now what will happen?" Aia said, and there was fear in her voice. "Now what bad things will come to us?"

I thought then that it was sad that in Aia's life there had been no new things that were good.

"All this time the Bushmen have been with the army because there were jobs there and there was pay to feed the children and to buy things. What will happen to them when the army goes and the new government looks at this thing and says, 'Haai! The Bushmen have been with our enemies!'? Yes. What will happen then?"

I saw again the fear in Aia's eyes and I heard it in her voice.

"They will come. Yes, they will come. And then who will look after us? I ask you. Who will look after us then?"

Kleinbaas too was afraid.

When I saw this I began to be frightened also. I saw

it on the day the white truck came with the big letters on the side saying UN. There was a lady and a man and they had blue hats and smiles.

"Good afternoon," she said to Kleinbaas. It was afternoon again on a day when rain should have fallen but didn't. Kleinbaas was worried that the small rain would pass right by that year. Every day we looked for rain but there were only clouds.

Kleinbaas said something I couldn't hear.

"We would just like to be sure that all your staff have registered to vote. That they know what to do." She smiled again. "Some of the people in the more outlying regions are a bit cut off and if they don't have radio or television . . ."

Kleinbaas didn't smile back at her. "My people know how they will vote, and when the time comes I will take them to register."

"But the time is now!"

"The time is when I say it is the time!"

For a moment the smiling lady stopped smiling and I thought that she could be hard too, if she wanted to.

"I'm afraid you are wrong there," she said firmly. "The people have a right to—"

"I'll take them," Kleinbaas said rudely, before she could finish. "Tomorrow."

And it was then, while the white truck with UN written on it, containing the people with the blue hats, was turning in the road, that I saw that Kleinbaas was afraid.

It didn't help when Khu also came to speak to Grandfather again that day. Kleinbaas grew red like a guinea fowl's neck.

"I told you," he said loudly, "that you were not allowed on this farm!"

Khu looked very cool. "I must speak to Dam and I would like"—his eyes flicked across to where I was standing—"to speak to Be as well."

I thought Kleinbaas was going to explode, right there in the middle of the farmyard.

"Get off my land," he said. "Now."

Khu turned to Grandfather, raising his arms helplessly. "You do realize," he said quietly, "that tomorrow is the last day that you can register to vote? The time has already been extended because there were so many people, but tomorrow is really the last day."

Grandfather looked quickly at Kleinbaas. I thought with a sense of shock that he was not going to answer, that he needed to ask permission first. I was ashamed of Grandfather at that moment. Ashamed that he had to ask. I felt the words rush up to my mouth before I could stop them.

"Yes! We know!" I said wildly. "The people from the UN came earlier today and the men before . . . with the flags, who gave us the T-shirts. We know. We really do!"

Kleinbaas looked at me then as if he had never seen me before. As if one of his cows had suddenly spoken—and he didn't like what it was saying.

"Yes," he said slowly, still watching me. "We know. I will be taking my people to Gobabis tomorrow."

Khu was already turning to go. "Good," he said. And then he smiled at me. "I will see you soon, Be."

Then he was gone.

Kleinbaas watched me while I walked across to the washing line to collect the clean clothes. I could feel his eyes on my back. It was a feeling I didn't like.

He took them the next day, all of them: Grandfather and Moses and Aia and the old Ovambo man and two of the Hereros who had been there when we came. The others had all gone: One had left because he said he wasn't paid enough; another because his wife was sick; one just disappeared overnight. None of them was replaced. Kleinbaas said the farm wasn't making enough money to waste on people who wouldn't work anyway. It was hard on Grandfather and Moses because they were both old.

"You," Kleinbaas said to me, "will stay with Mrs. Coetzee. She is not well enough to come with us." For a moment he looked into my eyes—something he never did—and I looked back. What did I see there? I try and try to find the words for the way Kleinbaas looked that morning. It wasn't anger or tiredness. It wasn't disinterest or suspicion or any look I had ever seen him give before. It was almost as if . . . as if he was pleading with me, asking me for something. Maybe he was.

Min and I watched the dust when they left.

"Would you like to brush my hair, Be?" Min was still very pale from her last headache, but cheerful. She didn't seem to be afraid of the elections and the new things that were coming. She smiled at me and I thought how pretty she was. The sun lit her bright hair from behind and her eyes were even bluer than usual.

"Yes, Mrs. Coetzee."

Brush and brush and brush, the silver-backed brush

moved through her hair as I worked and my thoughts were far away. With Khu.

"You love that boy, don't you, Be?"

I remember almost dropping the brush as my eyes looked at hers in the mirror. There was a moment when, for the first time, our minds met. Through our eyes, there in the mirror, our minds met. I saw Min. Min saw me.

"Yes," I said. This was no time to ask which boy she meant. No time to deny. No time to be silly and girlish. I felt like a woman, not a girl.

Min sighed. "I loved Mr. Coetzee, you know." Then she thought for a moment. "I *love* Mr. Coetzee."

I noticed that the brush had stopped moving.

"There was a time, Be, when he was not always angry." Her eyes were dreamy, like the mirror. "I expect you wonder. About how we came to marry. It was very romantic. Keep brushing, Be."

Brush and brush and her words kept time with the movement so that they dropped and rose like it did.

"I was in my third year. At University." Min's eyes were far away and dreamy, as if she was there again. "My father was so proud of me. Top student, I was, in my year. Pappa used to say I'd go far. Brilliant, he said." Her eyes sharpened again, holding mine. "He had it all mapped out for me. A year or so working in the field, to get experience, and then back to University and a job as a lecturer. Oh yes, it was all planned. Even professor, maybe."

And then I saw in Min's face how she must have looked when she was small.

"Only . . . only I didn't believe it would happen. I could see that he was going to be disappointed. So disappointed, Be." She looked at me anxiously. "And Pappa hadn't allowed at all for the idea that I might want to get married."

I wondered if I wanted to know this thing. I wondered if I wouldn't rather stay small and unknowing— and safe.

"Mr. Coetzee was so handsome. He came for the rugby, the big match between Cape Town and Stellenbosch Universities. I watched him play and then I met him at a dance afterward and we danced all evening together. He was so . . . so strong . . . so different from the boys I'd known before."

Min was looking right at me again. "I fell in love."

Yes. I could understand that.

"His father hated me . . . because I was different. Because I'd been to University. Because my father was an English liberal thinker. Mr. Coetzee's father said I had airs and graces above my station. He said that I came from a place that was nothing compared to what he could give his sons. Nothing!"

The glass ornaments on the dressing table shook a little at the anger in Min's voice.

"Oh, he was rich enough—but mean and spiteful at the same time! Farms in the Cape he had. Wine farms, a horse stud. Oh Be, you should have seen those horses—chestnuts and blacks, bays and dapple-grays— their long, thin legs flashing by, against the green of the grass."

She was quiet for a moment, thinking.

"He took us there, both of us, so we could see what we were missing, he said."

I felt then a small chill of . . . horror? Something like that. I sensed that what I was going to hear was horrible. And it was.

"There was a homestead that went with the horse farm—Persian carpets and golden, polished wooden floors. It was Christmas and the hydrangeas were all in bloom. Beautiful."

She was looking at me again. "Have you ever seen hydrangeas, Be?"

I shook my head.

"Well, it doesn't matter. He offered us lunch. Caviar. I don't suppose you've ever seen that either, Be? Well, it's a bit like champagne, only food—but I don't suppose . . ."

Her voice trailed away.

"And then there was roast lamb. I remember it well. And pink wine. And fresh peaches from the orchard, and coffee. And then, with the after-lunch liqueurs, he said—quite gently, as if it didn't really matter very much—that if Mr. Coetzee married me, he would have nothing. Nothing at all."

Min laughed then, a wild laugh. "So Mr. Coetzee stood right up and said to his father . . . Well, I don't suppose it's the kind of story I should be repeating to you, but he told him he could just keep his old horse farm and his silly old hydrangeas. *He* was going to keep *me*!"

For a while I brushed and Min sat quiet.

"That was before I got sick."

She was speaking slowly now, and the anger had gone from her.

"We lived in Port Elizabeth and Mr. Coetzee had a job at a motor-car factory. But he always wanted to be back on the farm—this farm, any farm! He used to come to Ontevrede when he was a boy. Every winter they all came here to hunt. Those were the days when they thought the game would last forever. When there were still elephant and lion and eland everywhere. Everywhere.

"Dam used to wait for them to come. He would wait in the place where they said, until he heard the sound of trucks crossing the veld, and then he would track for them for the hunting season. And they brought the meat back in a trailer, all salted and made into dry sausage for their friends in the Cape."

Brush and brush; brush and brush.

"So when the old man died and left Mr. Coetzee this farm after all he had said . . . Well, at first we had the idea that he had thought better of his words. It was only when we came here and found how neglected it was . . . nobody working—even old Dam was gone— the fences were down, the stock was missing, and there was no money. None at all. Not a single copper cent with which to build it all up."

I looked at Min in the mirror. And I saw her eyes turn from mirror to glass, so that I could see right into them, right into her. I saw that the madness was coming.

"It would have been better if we'd had some children. Sons to build for." Min laughed gaily. "But that was a problem as well. You know, of course, Be, that those dolls are my only children?"

Min gripped my wrist so hard that I had to stop brushing.

"You do know, of course, Be, that I'm a failure in that, too? Don't you, Be?"

I tried and tried to think of something to say. Something that would help.

"And it's not as if he hasn't had any others." Min's voice rose, like a little scream coming from her throat.

"There were other women—and their children too, although he tried to pretend they weren't his. So it's all my fault—as usual. No pretty horses, and no pretty children!"

"But he loves you!"

Min had been about to jump from the dressing table stool, I think, but she slowly sat down again.

"Does he, Be? Does he? Doesn't he love your mother instead?"

Her voice now was like a snake, coiled and ready to spring at my throat.

"No!" I whispered.

She held my eyes in her mirror.

"Yes."

And I knew it was true.

I don't remember what happened then.

My mind left me for a time, and when it came back the sky was dark, and the lights of the farm truck were coming up the road and I was caught in them like a spring hare and I could not move.

The bakkie stopped with a squeal of brakes and the door was flung open and Kleinbaas was standing there in the headlights, breathing like a bull and shouting.

"Be!"

He caught me in one hard hand and, as if I were a bag of rags, flung me against the wall.

"What the devil do you think you mean by this?"

He was waving a newspaper at me and I didn't understand. I didn't understand. The pages were falling out of his hands and he was spitting with anger.

"Turn my back for five minutes and Miss High-and-Mighty Bushman gives interviews to the newspapers.

The American newspapers! And everyone in Gobabis is talking about it since old Schmidt had the damn thing sent to him by his son in New York!"

Then Kleinbaas read from the newspaper, there in the light from the headlights, and I could see Aia's face, frightened in the half-dark behind him, and Grandfather with his hand over his eyes, shaking.

On the farm Ontevrede we met a shivering Bushman child who told us she worked for no wages, "but the madam gives me English lessons instead," and she lives on a diet of mealie porridge "because the frost killed the vegetables and there isn't enough money for meat." We saw the hovel where she and her mother live—no curtains and a narrow bed for the two of them. "We don't have any holidays, and I've never seen the sea"—this on the farm of Mr. Koos Coetzee in the Gobabis District. We can only hope that, when the elections are over, abuses such as these will come to a stop.

I thought Kleinbaas was going to kill me then.

"No!" I said. "It wasn't like that! That's not really what I said!"

"No!" and it was a great cry that came from Kleinbaas. "It isn't like that! It isn't like that! It never was like that. There isn't enough money, that's all. I meant to! I was going—when the heifers are sold, if there was enough—I was going to! It's not as if I ever . . ."

And then his eyes focused on me again and I saw the anger in them. Kleinbaas raised his fist as if he was going to do it. He was going to kill me. And then he stopped and his eyes seemed to see for the first time that there were no lights in the farmhouse and that the front door was open.

"Where's Mrs. Coetzee?" he shouted. "Where's my wife?"

I looked behind me. And I didn't know.

Morning. Another night has passed and I'm still here, still thinking, still alive.

I remember now that the hunters used to say that animals sometimes dragged themselves on for far longer than anyone could expect after the arrow brought its poison to them. Why? What is this will to live, in spite of everything? It's two days now and two nights. It must come soon. Death must come soon.

The veld is red-gold with the light of the new sun and the birds are stirring above me in the baobab. I saw a snake just now, a cobra. It looked at me and I looked at it, and then it passed on into the grass as if it had never been there, its smooth coils rippling away from me. Leaving me.

After Kleinbaas saw the open door he kind of sagged as if all the strength had gone out of him.

"Dam?" he said, and even his voice was weak. "Dam, she's gone." And the words fell flat on the ground, like stones.

Grandfather came toward us, trembling.

"Kleinbaas?"

Kleinbaas turned toward Grandfather, blind, like a mole in sudden light. "She's gone."

Then Grandfather did something I'd never expected to see. He put his hand on Kleinbaas and patted him, as a friend would. "We'll find her. We'll bring her back."

I remember the hardness of the wall behind me and of the stones under my legs, and my head was sore where I'd cracked it against the bricks. I remember Grandfather leading Kleinbaas away and saying something about torches and ropes, and then Aia was leaning over me.

"Be! Are you all right?"

Part of me wanted to bury my face in Aia and smell her smell and be her child again. Most of me remembered what Min had said.

"Don't touch me!" I said, and I heard my words like sharp, pointed knives.

Aia pulled away from me and I saw in the headlights, which still burned behind her, that she looked older suddenly, and afraid.

"Be . . ."

"Don't touch me!"

Because I knew it was true. I'd known it as soon as Min told me. Maybe I'd always known it, ever since we had come to Ontevrede: the looks and the looking away. The silences and the times in the night when Aia was gone. Yes. I'd known, somewhere in my mind. But because it was something I hadn't wanted to know . . . I'd pretended it wasn't there.

Pretend was a good game. When I was little. Pretend was escape from things you didn't want to think about. Pretend was something I'd learned from Aia.

71

And fear. What was it that Aia had always been afraid of?

"Why are you afraid?" I said it then. The question I'd always wanted to know the answer to.

I remembered Min saying to me: "You love that boy."

Aia looked like that. Like there was no pretence anymore. Like it was the end of the pretending. Like now I was old enough. And something inside me shouted: "You can go back! Just lean across and cry. Whimper like a baby and Aia will take you in her arms and it will be all right. It will! It will!"

But the time for that was gone.

"It started a long time ago," Aia said, and almost all the life had gone from her voice so that it was dull and flat like a well-used grinding stone. "It started when I was small. Like you were . . . once.

"Be, I don't know how to tell you this thing. I haven't been to school. I haven't learned to read books where you can find things that will help you to say what is in your heart. I only have my own words."

She looked at me, quite desperately then, and I found myself thinking, in the middle of her words, that I'd never tried to share my books—or my new thoughts— with Aia. That maybe I had made her afraid, too.

"Yes," I said.

"I think," and her voice was as far away as the stars, "that I was born at the wrong time. When I was a child my grandmother, my mother's mother, often used to talk to me. At night, when we sat together around the fire, she was the one who would tell me stories. I told the stories to you—but maybe you've forgotten."

It was as if Aia and I were settled there, as if we were around a fire that didn't burn. As if we were fixed there, in the light from the headlights of the truck, until this thing was settled between us. And Aia's voice went on and on, coming out of the darkness at me, nailing me to the wall.

"Grandmother was old—older than Dam. She remembered a long time ago, when our people lived in their own n!ores, and their n!ores were the whole of the Kalahari. She even remembered before that, when her grandmother had lived far to the south. When her grandmother's father had come from the high mountains that are in the east. Where it is hot, but the snow lies thick in winter."

The Drakensberg, I thought, and a picture came to my mind of Min's book, and the map that showed where the ancient cave painters had lived once. Maybe they hadn't been so ancient after all.

"I loved my grandmother. She used to hold me close under her kaross made of jackal skins and make me safe."

Aia's voice had changed. It was softer, dreamy.

"She used to make me look at the stars. 'Do you see that star?' she said to me once. 'That star is your cousin, Bau, who was killed by the lightning.' But when I was afraid, she laughed at my fears. 'Eh-hey!' she said, and her old laugh crackled across the empty veld behind our fire. 'That is the place to be, my girl! That's the place to be. Up there where the air is always cool and thin, and there is no hunger, and no thirst and you look down always on your people below and send them love. Send them your love.'

"Love, Be, that is the problem. Love. It twists us so

that we are not the same after it has come—and we can never be the same after it has gone."

For a moment Aia was quiet.

"My parents chose your father for me, Be. But when I saw him . . . Oh, he was beautiful, Be, beautiful. The best. He came for me when it was the time, and he brought meat and beads and honey . . . and love."

Aia looked directly at me, as if she wanted to tell me something with her eyes.

"That was the problem, Be. That was the problem. I loved your father too much. Too much." She stopped again as if the pain of it was unbearable, but then she whispered the beginning of the next part, until her voice grew stronger.

"But the time was wrong for him as well as for me. Our people were lost, Be, lost in the new things that we could not understand. We had lost our old way and we couldn't be a part of the new way. There was no land to hunt. No land to search for food from the veld. They took it. The government took it for the other people and for the Nature Conservation, until there wasn't enough for us. There were just jobs, and pay, so that we became eaters of money, and we were afraid.

"Your father didn't think he was lost. He had a job with the army, and he had good pay, so that we had tins of food and new blankets and plastic buckets to hold water. We had a radio, and your father had a watch, so that he knew when he was late.

"And he had money for drink, so that he looked away from me and saw other women, who laughed and danced and drank the strong drink that came from the shop. And he left me. He left us. He went with the other men who were lost. And one of them killed him with an axe that had been left out to chop the wood for the fire, so that he was dead, and he was really gone from us. From you, Be, and from me. Because of another woman."

Aia stood up then and a power was in her voice. "I swore then that I would never let that pain happen to me again. I would never love another man. Never!"

Her eyes blazed at me and were like stars.

"I would rather leave my place, and come to a far place, than let that happen to me again." She stared into the black for a while.

"So I did. When I saw that I might love again, a man at /Aotcha, my father's voice came to me out of the past and said that he needed me, so I left our place and I came here."

Before I could say anything, she went on: "And what I have here is not love. But pity and sorrow. And shame."

Aia turned away from me and walked into the darkness.

I didn't see her again.

◈ There was a time of pain: pain from my aching head; pain from my heart. What had I done? Kleinbaas had trusted me to look after Min. Aia had trusted me to love her. Grandfather had trusted me, too. Now they were gone, all gone, and the pain was too much for me to bear.

"Be!"

Somebody was shaking me.

"Be! You have to wake up!"

My body felt like a sigh that was being let out. So tired.

"*Be!*" Somebody shook me again. Hard. "Be. Wake up and tell me what's happened here!"

I opened my eyes, and there was Khu.

"Are you all right?"

I nodded.

"I'm sorry . . . I had to wake you . . . I thought . . ."

I knew what he had thought.

Khu helped me to sit up. I must have fallen away from the wall sometime while I was gone from myself. I felt that warmth of his arm under me. He smelled warm, too. Maybe he'd been running. I remembered what Aia had said, but I loved him still.

"What has been happening here?"

And then I saw what he must have seen: the truck lights blazing and the open door. There was a light in the kitchen now. Moths danced quietly in the light, and everything was still.

For a moment I just lay against Khu's arms and wished I could stay like that. Then I remembered Aia—and Min. Grandfather was out there somewhere, with his cough and his shaky legs. Min was missing. Min was mad. And Kleinbaas was nearly mad with grief and sorrow.

"It's . . ." And then I realized that it was time to be grown up. I think I shook myself, really shook myself, like a dog when it wakes up.

"Min . . . the farmer's wife . . . she's sick . . . very sick. They've gone to look for her. She ran away."

It wasn't everything, but it was enough for now. Aia I would worry about later.

Khu helped me to my feet. I held on to his hand and on to the moment as well as if I would never let go. But he was brisk now.

"I'll get the searchlight from the truck."

I saw then that the red four-wheel drive was parked behind the farm truck.

"You get some food . . . bread, anything. We'll go and see if we can help."

I made some sandwiches. Min liked sandwiches. Once, when Kleinbaas was away at the village, we'd been for a picnic, just the two of us, Min and I, a magic picnic, Min said, down in the kloof, where there was sometimes water and it was sometimes green. We'd taken apples and ginger beer and sandwiches. I took some butter from the paraffin fridge, and sliced some bread. It wasn't too stale. I made coffee too, with plenty of sugar, the way Min liked it, and poured it into the thermos flask. I picked up Min's warm shawl from the back of her chair. She might need it.

Khu was watching me from the doorway. "Is there a first-aid kit? Did they take it with them?"

They hadn't. It was still in the pantry where it always was.

"Have you got shoes?"

I shook my head. I'd be better without.

"A warm jersey? It's cold."

I fetched my jersey from our room. Aia wasn't there.

"Let's go!" And then he looked at me closely. "Are you sure you're all right?"

I looked back. Khu was a head taller than me and wider, stronger.

"Yes," I said.

I knew, really I knew, before we went, that Min was gone. Making the sandwiches, making the coffee the way she liked, with the sugar, bringing her warm shawl . . . it was a game, a make-believe.

We could see long before we got to the kloof. Kleinbaas had taken the big blue torch he used for the early-morning milking and Grandfather was holding it while Kleinbaas pulled the body up with the rope from the old plough. So small she looked, and her yellow hair hung down behind her and her arms and legs, twisted and flopping like one of her dolls. I was crying before we reached them.

Khu helped. Kleinbaas needed his help as he was almost finished. His big body had not been enough for him. His face was gray with exhaustion and his pale blue socks hung down around his ankles.

Nobody spoke.

Grandfather and Kleinbaas carried Min home between them, and Khu and I came behind. He put his arm around me and I leaned against him and I thought, I will take this warmth and this caring now, although I know I do not deserve it. I will take it now. And I will remember it always.

I remember . . . I remember emptiness. Nothing. Nothing. Nothing.

Aia was gone. Nobody knew where. She had taken her few things and just vanished into the dark. Grandfather coughed more, but he was all right. All right, I think.

There was a funeral and the people came all the way from Gobabis village, although none had come before while I had been there. The man came from the church too, and prayed while Kleinbaas and Grandfather and Moses lowered the coffin into the small, dry grave.

Kleinbaas told me to make food for the people. I made sandwiches with the special tin of ham Min had been keeping for Christmas. I thought she would have liked that. They ate them, and drank the wine Kleinbaas brought out from the cellar under the kitchen, and then they went home, and their trucks left lines behind them in the dust.

I didn't want any more secrets, but I got them anyway. Oh, Be, stirrer of the mealie porridge pot, once you have stirred, the bubbles rise to the surface.

"You are very like your mother." That was Grandfather, the day after the funeral. "Very like her." And then, more gently, "She will come back, you know. She will come back." But I didn't think so.

Stories, stories, the past is just so many stories and there is no escape from them, and no escape from the past either.

"Kleinbaas . . . you know he is my friend?" Grandfather didn't wait for me to answer. "When I left that place . . . well, I was empty. There was nothing there. All I could think of was to get away, and the only place I knew was here, Ontevrede, where I had lived before."

Grandfather shook his head slowly, remembering. "I don't suppose you know how the farm got its name? No, I don't suppose you do. Do you even know what it means? Ontevrede means 'not enough.' Not being happy with what you have . . . with what you are . . . with what you get." He gave a short, bitter laugh. "It's as good a name as any for this farm. Oubaas—the father of Kleinbaas—chose it."

I could feel Grandfather looking at me, waiting for me to say something, but I had nothing to tell him.

"Be . . . you are an important person in my heart. I want you to understand. I want you to . . . know what it was like for me."

Still I was silent.

Grandfather shrugged, hopelessly. "I am old. That was my life. That was the way it was for me, and soon it will be over. I lived and lived, and now I am old. I know about many things, things I have seen and things people have spoken of, but I do not remember how it is to be young."

I looked at Grandfather then. His eyes were sad and dark, like pools of rainwater in a long night. "No," he said, and then he smiled. "I don't remember, but I expect I had to learn when it was my time."

He was silent for a while. Then he reached over and touched my arm with his worn, thin hand. "Be . . . Oh, my granddaughter, is it then so heavy?"

When I didn't answer—when I couldn't answer—he went on anyway. Talking about other things. Trying to make me think about other things.

"The old man—Oubaas—now, there was a man. Hunted everything that moved in the old days, when we were both young. I used to track for him, up north. Elephant, lion . . . it was the elephant, you know, that paid for the farm."

I must have looked totally blank because Grandfather laughed again, and this time it was a good laugh.

"The old man wasn't as unfeeling as he liked to make out. He had his ways, all right. Plenty of them. But he'd never have seen Kleinbaas starve. Or his wife either. Or me. He left this place to Kleinbaas because he was angry about the marriage to the English-woman—and left him to figure out how to make a go of it, too! But there was a kind of insurance policy as well. That was me!"

Grandfather looked so pleased with himself that I had to smile. A small smile.

"I knew where the ivory was, that's what!"

Grandfather still looked as pleased as he must have done all those years ago, I thought.

"Of course, where it all went wrong was when Mrs. Coetzee got sick." Grandfather had stopped smiling now. "And Oubaas wasn't to know that I'd . . . well, that things would be bad for me. Oubaas thought I would always want to stay here. He never knew I'd gone back. But I didn't stay gone. And the ivory was still there, where we'd hidden it, Oubaas and me.

"Kleinbaas and I used to get a tusk or two every time

81

the money ran out—slowly, slowly, so that the price would still stay high. And every time we sold some ivory, we bought something for Ontevrede. A stud bull or a new welder or some fencing wire. It would have made Oubaas smile to see that.

"Yes." Grandfather stopped again, as if he'd run out of electricity, like the generator did when the petrol was finished. "It's dangerous to meddle out of your time. Oubaas was playing games with us all. With our lives." For a moment he looked up, as if Oubaas might be watching him still, to see how it had all worked out. "Yes. Unhappiness is a thing you cannot see in the future. Maybe that is as well. Yes. Maybe that is as well."

I felt his hand on my hair. "Pretty, Be. Did you know that? Beautiful, maybe."

Behind him he left the small wind of his going.

And what was there for me after that? Me, Be of the Ju/'hoan, whom some call the Bushman? I will tell you what there was. Nothing.

I went the next day, before Kleinbaas could forget his sorrow and get angry again about the newspaper report and about . . . about betraying him. Before Aia could return to haunt me. Aia was like a ghost already, from the past. Before Grandfather could die of TB. Before . . .

Yes, most of all, before Khu could find out that I was nothing, nothing, and worse than nothing. I had disappointed everybody, even myself. Yes. Before he could find that out.

Because there had been . . . something. The warmth of Khu was not just—and I knew, in my mind, that this was really true—not just sympathy. The warmth of

Khu was something that I could take for my own, because it had been just for me. Before he knew. Before he found out. I could keep that.

So I went.

But before I left, I looked at Min's book. The book where it had started. I was a Bushman. I wanted to read what a Bushman was.

These people are distinguished by their strange, almost incomprehensible language and their unusual stature. There is some talk that they may come, originally, from Asia, because of their narrow eyes.

I looked at my narrow eyes in Min's mirror. They wanted, these people who wrote books, to take away even our Africa from us.

Males of the species are short of stature, usually about five feet tall, and females are shorter and broader because they store more fat.

I felt the anger begin to burn in me then. *Males, females.* This was like the book about dinosaurs that Min had once brought for me. *The brontosaurus was a meat eater, we imagine, because of his teeth.* I bared my teeth at Min's mirror. Small and white. Would they say, these people who wrote books, that I was a ham-sandwich eater? One day when they dug up my head and found my teeth?

Distinguished by apricot-colored skin and peppercorn hair.

To blazes with the writers of books! *My* skin was skin and *my* hair was hair.

An unusually integrated lifestyle, relying to an exceptional degree on nature.

I took the book and I threw it at the mirror. The shattering of the glass was one of the most satisfying sounds I've ever heard. But I thought of Min. She had known. Really, she had. Min had known that I wasn't just a "female of the species with apricot-colored skin and peppercorn hair."

Then I left.

It was a long way. Back was a long way, but it was the only way I could think to go.

The hard part was remembering Aia all the way. I needed the things she had taught me. I needed to be a Bushman. I needed what all the people who had gone before had taught me.

It was knowing when the small, three-cornered leaves appeared that there were bulbs underneath that could quench my thirst. It was knowing what to do with the bulb when I'd dug it up. It was being able to light my evening fire and know which sticks to put on it that would last through the night in case the lions came. It was finding the beans that take the edge away from hunger. It was building my shelter so that it faced the right way, so that the chill night wind sighed without making me cold. It was a thousand things.

Nothing I had learned in the schoolbooks with Min was of the slightest use. Not one thing. I worried about that a lot. What was the point? Why had I bothered to learn to read and count if there was no use in it all?

I was not going to need any of it. Ever again.

I came to /Aotcha on an autumn day when the bush was golden, honey-golden.

I knew the place. Knew it by the giant baobab tree, long before I got there. And my heart began to fall inside me. What would I find there? Would Aia be there? Would Khu? Would he want to see me? And, worst of all, would Khu be happy in a small shelter with a wife, and babies and children, smiling at me? Would Aia be happy? My mind began to say to me that this wasn't going to work either.

My feet walked slower and slower as I passed the wind pump and the well-remembered path. This was where I had walked that day with old Xama and Nisa, that day and many days.

The birds swirled out of the top branches and their cries were harsh. "Go away," I thought they said. "Go away. Your place is not here!" A small ground-squirrel ran across my path and he stopped to look back at me with his sharp, unfriendly eyes.

It was too hot to go on. Too hot to walk the last space. I would wait here, at the baobab, until something happened.

Its trunk was warm behind my back. This tree had been here in the old days, when my people first came to this n!ore. It had seen them come and it would see them go. There was nothing that I, Be, could do to stop whatever would happen. I saw them standing behind me, my people, in a long, straight line leading to nowhere. The old, old people with their leather tied around their waists and their far-seeing eyes looking for the eland that now was gone. Aia's grandmother with her stories and her laughter. Grandfather pulling

85

his mother out of the drinking fire, and Aia . . . Aia, who was too afraid to love. And at the end of them all I saw me. I saw Be of the Ju/'hoan, and I was the last of them all.

It came to me then that I was too tired to go on to /Aotcha camp. I was too tired to work it through until the end. For what would the end be?

But I made myself get up from the foot of the tree and I made myself go on, those last few hundred steps that took me to /Aotcha camp. Who was I to decide? Let me see what was there before I gave up.

There was nobody.

I wandered around a bit and my feet made sad tracks behind me as I went. The sun was long at my back as I walked, and the shadows of it black. Soon it would be night.

Old Kamha's hut still had the bicycle hanging outside it in the tree, I saw, and there were still the old bottles and plastic bags and tins everywhere that had been there before we went. Tushay was still making arrows. He must have been making some before he left so suddenly. There were seven of them balanced on a log of wood so that the poison tips could dry in the sun. I took one, I wasn't sure why, and put it carefully in my carrying bag.

The ash of the fires was still warm, so they hadn't been gone long. What could have happened to make them all leave so suddenly? Something bad.

Someone had left blankets hanging over a bit of old barbed wire. They'd built a kraal for the cattle since I'd been here, but there were no cows, only a few dirty puppies playing near the gate.

It was the same, the same, the same as it would always be.

I turned away and walked back toward the big baobab.

I don't know when the idea became something complete inside my mind, but it was before I got to the tree. If I turned right, I would find the road to Tsumkwe. If I went left, I would come to /Aotcha Pan, where I had never been before. I'd been too small to go with the older children who sometimes crossed the pan.

"Don't wander away!" the big people told us. "There are animals out there," and we believed them.

But now my feet took that way. The pan shimmered ahead of me in the last light, butter-brown and gold in the light, and the sand was soft under my feet. A jackal ran in front of me, its glowing eyes more frightened by far than mine. There was only a little water in the pan. The rains here had not been good.

My footsteps took me away, away from that place, across the pan to where the wild was.

8

⬧ The wind came then, howling down on me like a mad animal, whirling the sand into great clouds that blotted out the sun. I walked bent forward into it and my eyes stung with dust and my head ached with the pain of it. Before I had gone very far, the village and the baobab and the wind pump were lost as if they had never been, and there was just me, in a dark wilderness of dust and a screaming wind.

"Where are you going, Be?" I asked myself out loud, but the wind took my words and threw them into the desert and the answer came back to me. "Nowhere." I think it was then that I realized why I had stolen Tushay's poison arrow. Night came, but the dust still sang in my ears and I walked, one foot in front of the other, and my mind was closed.

Maybe there were lions. Certainly there were other animals, lost like me in the storm of dust and wind, but I didn't care about them. I walked and walked all night until I had crossed the pan and the scream of the wind sank to a whisper and the dust dropped. Then I found a place where there was some shade from a small thorn tree and lay down on the bare ground with my blanket pulled over my head, and I slept.

* * *

*It is very still, here in the veld. Ants hurry silently
past my foot, busy with important things. The sun is
hot, hot on the back of my neck, and the air is heavy
with rain that doesn't fall. This morning I was sitting
so quiet and still that a small buck walked almost
onto me and stood for a second looking straight into
my eyes as if it couldn't believe what it was seeing.
Then it was gone with a quick flick of its white tail
and I was even lonelier than I had been before.*

*Maybe that's because of the footprint. How do I
know it was his footprint? I knew. It was a long, slen-
der foot, strong. He had been running. It was Khu. I
saw it this morning and I know it was not there in
that place yesterday when I passed.*

*I'm sure now that the poison is working. I'm very
weak and my legs shake if I try to walk. I should
drink some water. The ostrich shell is still almost full,
but I am too tired to walk over to get it.*

*It comes to me now that these are the last thoughts
I will think. Aia. Aia and Khu. Grandfather and Min.*

I loved them.

There is a voice, speaking to me. There is a sound I
recognize—wood being cut? Yes, a knife on wood, carving. There is the smell of rain, the smell that the rain
makes on the dust. The ground under me is very hard.

It is Khu.

"It took a long time, Be, a long time to track you. Because of the wind. Your footsteps were blown away. We
were waiting for you to come. Your mother said you
would come. We went for you, Be, to bring you back.
After your mother had come from the Gobabis Dis-

trict, with the cattle truck and the headmaster's bakkie. Tushay said we must bring you home so that you could live with your mother and him."

The knife scraped and scraped on the wood.

"They care about you, Be. Very much."

I thought of Aia and Tushay, who was the man she had not wanted to love. A good man.

"We went right to the farm and only your grandfather and Mr. Coetzee were there, dipping the cattle. They said you had gone. They said you had taken your things and left and they didn't know where you were going. So we came back to wait for you at /Aotcha."

I thought of Grandfather and Kleinbaas just going on, and going on, and of how there were only the two of them now, and maybe Moses, if he was still there.

"First we looked on the road to Tsumkwe. After we saw that you had been in the village."

How had they known that?

"We saw that you had taken the arrow of Tushay and we found one footstep that was left. Just that one, where you had stepped inside Old Xama's hut, and of course I knew that it was you."

Sometimes the voice goes away and there is just the sound of the scraping and carving of the wood. Sometimes everything is still and quiet, a cool breeze crosses my face, and I listen and listen, my eyes still tightly closed, and I imagine that I can hear the stars sighing in the night sky above me. There is water that he gives me, sip by sip, and the warmth of his arm under my head, behind my neck.

* * *

90

"Oh, Be," he said. "You will be pleased when you hear what has happened!"

And then he seemed to think of something else.

"Do you remember that day when I first came to the farm?"

Did I remember?

"You were coming out of the cow shed and marching across the farmyard with your head down, like a . . . I don't know, like a beautiful young eland with her mind made up about something."

Beautiful. He thought I was beautiful.

"And when I spoke you jumped like a spring hare! And your eyes were huge in your face. I don't think you drew breath for the next five minutes."

He remembered.

Khu laughed a small laugh. "I knew you would be there that day. My mother had spoken of you. I came to see what you were like."

His mother had spoken of me. He had come to see . . .

"Can you hear me yet, Be?"

I couldn't answer him. I was too weak even to smile.

"You will get better soon—you will. You must just keep taking water."

And then he came over from where he'd been sitting and gave me some more to drink. Some of it trickled down my neck, but I could feel the rest of it, cool as night, slipping over my dry throat.

"When you can walk again, I'll take you back to /Aotcha."

For a moment he was very busy with his knife on the wood. I heard the chips of falling wood.

"And maybe . . . if you like . . . I mean if you want to . . . later, we could . . . I'll speak to Tushay and your

91

mother." Again he was silent. My ears strained toward him.

"I mean, it's time I took a wife."

After that was a warm time when I lay cocooned in my own happiness. I didn't understand. I didn't care. Somehow Khu believed that I wasn't going to die, and he loved me. That was enough to hear for that time.

". . . and then, after I'd finished Standard Seven, I came back to the village, to see what was happening there. When I was far away . . . well, I missed /Aotcha. I missed my own people. And then it was the time when the people were beginning to see that they couldn't just stay in their own n!ores and pretend that the outside didn't exist."

He carved away, silent for a while.

"It's no use trying to go back, back in time, back to an old life that doesn't—that can't—exist anymore. The old people were glad when they heard that I, and others of the young people, wanted to stay. Yes, they told us, we need you.

"Then we went to the other villages, all of us, the old people and the young people who wanted to speak, to the other n!ores, and brought them news.

"Oh, Be! What times there are ahead for us! The best of times. For too long now we have been speaking as people who do not believe in themselves. Who do not have their own n!ore and their own right to be there and to raise their voice to be heard.

"This thing, this speaking out, began with the Farmers' Cooperative and has grown so that now we are listened to. Ministers come, from the new government, to talk to us and on the day when you came to /Aotcha the new President came himself to listen to us.

"Do you hear that, my Be? If you can't, I will tell you again, and again, until you know this thing as well. All of us from the village went on the trucks and we waited at the old Baobab in Tsumkwe until the President came to talk to us.

"Oh Be, isn't it wonderful that we Ju/'hoan are at last being heard and our words are going even to the high places of our land, and the President of all Namibia came with his wife and his advisers to see for himself? Yes, Be. He came himself and this was the first time such a thing has happened, although it will not be the last."

Night again. Khu put the kaross over me and stroked my cheek. I felt the warmth of his fingers and I tried to speak, to say something, but I felt as though a great weight was in me, like iron, and my voice couldn't speak. The night was not gone when Khu came back. He was shaking—I could feel that, and he was afraid.

"Be! My Be! If you can hear me, hear these words. I know you think that the arrow you took was poisoned—and I have seen the place where you . . . but, Be, it was not, it was not! What hunter would leave poisoned arrows where a child might find them? Or a frightened girl? You mustn't die! You can't die. Not now, when everything is beginning."

Khu rubbed my hands, my wrists, giving me his warmth.

"I thought now—I was asleep—but I thought you were going. I thought you were slipping away while I slept. I felt your heart, in my dream, beating slower and slower and I saw, in my dream, that you had left me before I had time to tell you . . . I never told you, not in real words. I love you, my Be. I love your spirit and your heart and your eyes, and when the new times begin I want you to be with me to meet them."

All the time he was speaking, Khu rubbed my hands between his own and somewhere, inside, the warmth came to my heart.

"I love you, Be."

I thought that maybe I could open my eyes again.

The smoke in the flames
of the fires of Bushmanland.
The honey-gold of the grass
and the wind singing through.
The scent of sweetness on the air
and the soft, gray dust
—before our footsteps
were blown out.

About the Author

Lesley Beake was born in Scotland and has lived in various parts of Africa and the Middle East. While writing textbook material for Ju'/hoan (Bushman, or San) children, she traveled to the remote parts of the Kalahari Desert. There she met several young women who inspired her story of Be.

Lesley Beake lives in South Africa, where she has won many awards for her writing.